NATIONAL GEOGRAPHIC KiDS

weird but true!

know-it-all

Greek Mythology

THE TEMPLE OF POSEIDON, BUILT AROUND 440 B.C., HONORS THE GOD OF THE SEA. PERCHED ON THE EDGE OF A CLIFF, THE MARBLE TEMPLE IS SURROUNDED BY THE SPARKLING BLUE WATER OF SOUNION BAY.

NATIONAL GEOGRAPHIC KiDS

weird but true! ....

know-it-all

Greek Mythology

SARAH WASSNER FLYNN
ILLUSTRATED BY CHIP WASS

NATIONAL GEOGRAPHIC

SCHOLASTIC INC.

CONTENTS

OH MY... GODS!

Welcome to the wild, wacky, and wonderful world of Greek mythology. Passed down from generation to generation, these stories—or myths—originated thousands of years ago as a way for ancient Greeks to understand what was going on in their lives and in the world around them. Things like astronomy, biology, meteorology, and other sciences were still centuries away from being developed, so the ancient Greeks came up with stories to explain it all. The change in seasons? The creation of the planet? The reason your voice echoes when you yell into a canyon? Yep, there's a myth for *all* of that.

The ancient Greeks used myths to answer life's other tough questions, too, like where people go after they die. They taught valuable lessons, like the importance of being brave and of choosing good over evil. Myths often were a vehicle for retelling historical events, including stories of real-life battles and wars.

Greek myths are mostly fictional. But the ancient Greeks lived by them as though they were the real deal. To them, myths weren't just stories, but a religion. They worshipped the Gods and built temples to them—and the ruins of some still stand! These stories were a major part of their everyday lives—so powerful that they are still super popular today.

THERE'S A MYTH FOR THAT

Here's how the ancient Greeks explained certain natural phenomena.

FIRE

THE MYTH: The god Prometheus stole fire from the gods and gave it to humans, bringing them light, warmth, and the power to cook their food.

EARTHQUAKES

THE MYTH: The earth shook every time Poseidon, the god of the sea, crashed his trident to the ground.

SUNSET & SUNRISE

THE MYTH: The god Helios pulled the sun in a golden chariot. Each day, he'd drive the chariot along the sky, causing the sun to rise and set.

IT'S MYTHIC!

Some ancient Greeks wouldn't eat beans because they thought they contained the souls of the dead.

VOLCANIC ERUPTIONS

THE MYTH: Hephaestus set off eruptions each time he created something new in his fiery workshop beneath a volcano.

THUNDERSTORMS

THE MYTH: An angry Zeus would hurl lightning bolts, thunder, and rain down to Earth.

THE SEASONS

THE MYTH: Demeter, the goddess of the seasons and agriculture, created the seasons after her daughter Persephone was kidnapped by Hades and taken into the Underworld for six months of the year. While her daughter was away, Demeter created an endless winter.

PASS IT DOWN

The ancient Greeks couldn't Snapchat or text their friends, or share stories by posting pics online. So how did the myths make their way to us over thousands of years? People talked! Some ancient Greek people passed myths down verbally, while others wrote them down. The system wasn't perfect, though. Like a game of telephone, the stories were altered over time as people shared them. That's why there's often more than one version of the same myth.

GODS: THEY'RE JUST LIKE US

Well, *kind* of. Sure, they had superpowers that no person could ever possess (shape-shifting and immortality, anyone?), but in many ways they were similar to regular people. After all, the ancient Greeks based these fictional characters on humans ... with a twist. Most of them looked like men and women, and had certain character traits based on human nature, like jealousy, anger, and fear. They got married and had families. Also, many of them loved to eat good food, listen to music, hang out with friends, and have parties. Hmm, sound familiar?

yaas, #winning

HEROES' WELCOME

Gods and goddesses aren't the only characters to star in Greek myths. Mythology also tells tales of great mortal heroes who completed daunting and daring tasks—making them superstars among the gods. From fighting ferocious monsters to slaying on the battlefield, these heroes personified courage and strength. They may have been totally accomplished, but these heroes weren't without their flaws: Some were hot-headed, jealous, and selfish. And this, experts believe, is the ancient Greeks' way of reminding us that, well, *nobody's* perfect.

GREEK MYTHOLOGY

BY THE NUMBERS

3
The number of heads possessed by Cerberus, the watchdog of the Underworld.

10
The number of years it took the hero Odysseus to return home after the Trojan War, as told in the epic poems *The Iliad* and *The Odyssey* by famed poet Homer.

12
The number of gods who lived on Mount Olympus, also known as the Olympians.

700 B.C.
The year the famous poet Hesiod published *Theogony*, the first written documented story of Greek mythology.

9
The number of Muses mentioned in Greek mythology. These were the goddesses who inspired artists, musicians, dancers, and writers.

GREEK OUT!

They may have been written long ago, but ancient Greek myths have had a lasting effect. Here's how myths and the gods they focus on factor into our everyday lives.

MYTHS ON THE MAP

Cities and towns that take their names from Greek mythology

HADES CREEK, WASHINGTON

ECHO, OREGON

HERCULES, CALIFORNIA

URANUS, ALASKA

ARES PEAK, NEW MEXICO

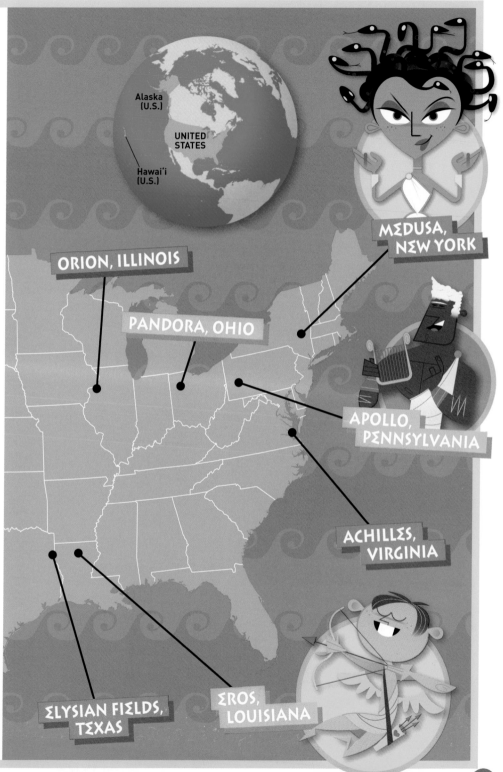

GOD-GIVEN WORDS

Say what? These common words have mythic roots.

HYGIENE

THE MEANING: Personal care and cleanliness

THE GOD: Hygeia, goddess of good health

HYPNOSIS

THE MEANING: To put into a sleep-like state

THE GOD: Hypnos, god of sleep

IRIDESCENT

THE MEANING: Displaying a sheen of lustrous, rainbow-like colors

THE GOD: Iris, goddess of the rainbow

PSYCHIC

THE MEANING: A person who is sensitive to supernatural forces

THE GOD: Psyche, goddess of the soul

PHOBIA

THE MEANING: A fear

THE GOD: Phobos, god of fear

NEMESIS

THE MEANING: A rival or enemy

THE GOD: Nemesis, goddess of divine retribution (she took revenge against humans who went against the gods)

MUSEUM

THE MEANING: A building where objects of artistic, historical, cultural, or scientific interest are housed and exhibited

THE GOD: The nine Muses

Here are some fan-favorite fictional figures with close ties to Greek mythology.

HERMIONE GRANGER

THE SOURCE: The Harry Potter book series by J.K. Rowling

THE STORY: The beloved Harry Potter heroine's name is plucked from mythology; Hermione (which means "dedicated to Hermes") was the daughter of Helen of Troy and the king of Sparta.

SHAZAM

THE SOURCE: *Shazam!* the movie

THE STORY: The Marvel superhero is said to have the abilities of six mythological figures, including the strength of Heracles, the stamina of Atlas, and the power of Zeus.

PERCY JACKSON

THE SOURCE: Percy Jackson and the Olympians book series by Rick Riordan

THE STORY: The books reimagine Greek mythology in a modern era, chronicling Perseus "Percy" Jackson and his friends' journeys that mirror the ones you read about in myths.

MEG

THE SOURCE: Disney's *Hercules*

THE STORY: In both the Greek myth *and* the classic animated film, the sassy and smart Meg (short for Megara) is rescued by the hero Hercules (aka Heracles)— and the two soon fall in love before she faces an untimely death.

THESE MYTHS MEAN BUSINESS

Some of the world's most recognized brands borrowed their names from Greek mythology.

WE ARE THE CHAMPIONS. Back when it launched in 1971, **NIKE** drew on the goddess of victory to give the brand a winning vibe.

CHEW ON THIS. Popping a piece of **TRIDENT** won't give you power over the seas, but it will make your breath fresh! The popular packs of minty gum share a name with Poseidon's giant three-pronged weapon.

CLEAN UP. It's fitting that **AJAX**, the "stronger than dirt" cleaner, has the same name as a legendary Greek hero. The grandson of Zeus, the powerful Ajax played a pivotal role in the Trojan War.

ROAD TRIP. The name given to this top-selling model of minivan, the Honda **ODYSSEY**, inspires drivers to take their own epic journeys—albeit a bit less eventful than Odysseus's!

Gaea & Uranus

MOTHER EARTH & FATHER HEAVEN

CLAIM TO FAME

Together, they created the Titans, the first gods and goddesses on Earth.

WHY THEY'RE WEIRD This couple produced the Cosmic Egg, which contained the Earth and the sea.

OUT OF THE DARK

What was life like at the very beginning of time? Ancient Greek mythology explains it as a dark, empty abyss called Chaos. This was a place of nothingness: No sun, no moon, no stars. But out of Chaos eventually came something awesome: the Earth. Actually, it was a goddess named Gaea (pronounced "Jee-uh" or "Gay-uh"), the spirit of the Earth as it formed from Chaos.

Gaea first emerged from the darkness on her own, alone and dry as a desert with nothing living on her. It wasn't until she looked up into the sparkling stars and locked eyes on Uranus, the ruler of the sky, that things began to get a little more lively. Instantly smitten, Uranus sent rain showers from his perch in the sky down onto Gaea, forming the first lakes and seas on Earth. Soon, plants began to grow and Gaea bloomed with lush valleys, towering trees, and soaring mountains.

hello, world!

rude!

TRIPLE THREAT

United in love, Gaea and Uranus welcomed several children. Their first six kids included two sets of triplets, but this brood wasn't your typical bunch of bouncing babies with 10 fingers and 10 toes. They were all giants, standing taller than the mountains. One set of triplets was born with 50 heads and 100 powerful arms each (imagine counting all of those fingers!). The other was a trio of one-eyed Cyclopes—called Lightning, Thunder, and Thunderbolt—with enough strength to rival the forces of nature they were named for. While Gaea loved all of her children endlessly and equally, Uranus wanted nothing to do with them. He called them ugly and did not believe they deserved to exist on the beautiful planet. So he seized all six of them and flung them into the darkest, deepest pit under the earth, a place called Tartarus.

WHO ARE YOU CALLING A MONSTER?

They had faces—and limbs—only a mother could love, literally. Among Gaea and Uranus's 12 children, three of them were Hecatoncheires, or "100-handers." Massive beasts with 50 heads and, yes, 100 arms, these giants stirred fear in nearly everyone they encountered, including their own father. But even though Uranus tossed them in Tartarus, they didn't stay there forever. They were eventually freed and played a role in helping Zeus, the king of gods, overthrow the early gods.

anybody up there?

IT'S SAID THAT **GAEA** FORMED THE EARTH'S **RIVERS** AND **CREEKS** BY **OPENING UP HER VEINS** AND LETTING **WATER RUSH OUT.**

STONE COLD

While Gaea went on to have six more children, her love for Uranus was forever tainted. She continued to mourn the imprisonment of her firstborn children. When Cronus, from her second batch of sons, became old enough, she asked him to go after Uranus with a sickle made of adamant, a mythical, unbreakable rock. Doing as he was told, Cronus attacked Uranus, who could not compete with his superpowered son—or his weapon. He fled, and Cronus became the new lord of the universe.

IT'S MYTHIC!

A supercomputer used by the National Oceanic and Atmospheric Administration (NOAA) to predict patterns in climate change is named Gaea, after the goddess.

MODERN MYTHOLOGY WRITTEN IN THE STARS

It's no coincidence that the seventh planet in our solar system shares a name with Uranus, the ancient god of the heavens. But it was actually the Romans, not the Greeks, who first named the five planets closest to the sun—Mercury, Venus, Mars, Jupiter, and Saturn—after their most beloved gods. Two thousand years ago, these were the only orbs visible from Earth. It wasn't until the invention of telescopes that astronomers discovered the remaining two official planets, Uranus and Neptune. They kept up the tradition of drawing from gods for inspiration, but went Greek, not Roman, to name Uranus.

The Titans

WHO'S WHO AMONG THE TITANS

With a group of 12 siblings, it's tough to keep track of everyone! Here's a breakdown of each of the Titans' titles.

RHEA

The queen of the Titans, she was also known as the mother of gods.

THEIA

The Titan goddess of gold, silver, and other glittering jewels, she was also known as the mother of the sun and the goddess of vision.

COEUS

One of the most inquisitive Titans, his name means "query" or "questioning."

OCEANUS

The big brother of the bunch, he ruled over the oceans. Some works of ancient art show him as part man, part sea serpent.

TETHYS

The first goddess of rivers and freshwater. She was married to her brother Oceanus.

WHY THEY'RE WEIRD

This set of 12 siblings were each taller than a mountain.

FAMILY MATTERS

These super-siblings go way back! The 12-pack of brothers and sisters—six girls and six boys—represented the generation before the Olympian gods in Greek mythology. In fact, if it wasn't for the Titans,

HYPERION

Hello, sunshine. With a name meaning "he who watches from above," Hyperion was known as the god of sunlight.

IAPETUS

The god of mortality, he presided over the timeline of all mortals.

CRIUS

The god of the constellations, he was in charge of ordering the measures of the year.

PHOEBE

The goddess of the moon, her name means "bright" or "shining."

MNEMOSYNE

With a name that means "memory" in Greek, you can't forget this goddess of teachers.

CRONUS

The youngest of the Titans. He became their leader after leading the charge to overthrow their father, Uranus. Married to Rhea, they had a famous brood that included Zeus and Poseidon.

THEMIS

She presided over law and order and justice.

CLAIM TO FAME
The Titans ruled the Earth until they were overthrown by Zeus and the Olympian gods.

there'd be no Zeus, Poseidon, Athena, or any of the other famous gods and goddesses we know about today. The Titans were giants in every way: Ancient art depicts these immortals as mega-size, each equipped with magical and mystic powers. Together, they ruled over Greece from atop Mount Othrys.

Rhea & Cronus

MOTHER & FATHER OF THE GODS

CLAIM TO FAME

They were the parents of the most powerful Greek gods and goddesses.

WHY THEY'RE WEIRD

Rhea stayed with Cronus even after he ate some of their kids.

UNHAPPILY EVER AFTER

A match made in the heavens? Not quite. While Rhea and Cronus may have been the picture of marital bliss at first, their union ultimately fizzled. And for good reason. After a prophet warned him that his five children, who were gods, would one day overthrow him just as he did to his own father, Cronus chose to do something drastic: He swallowed them. (But don't worry: The children weren't gone for good. They eventually, um, came back up.)

yum

ROCK BOTTOM

When she found out she was expecting her sixth child, a fearful Rhea wanted to get away from her power-hungry husband. With the help of her mom, Gaea, Rhea snuck away one night and wound up hiding out in a cave tucked inside a mountain. There, she eventually welcomed Zeus. Knowing Cronus would find her, Rhea returned to her husband with a trick up her sleeve. She wrapped up a baby-size rock in a blanket and handed it to her husband. Cronus promptly gulped it down, satisfied that his position as lord of the universe would remain firmly in place.

#CAVELIFE

Meanwhile, cave life continued for Zeus, who was being looked after by nymphs and a goat named Amaltheia, while Rhea pretended to mourn the baby lost inside her husband's belly. Gaea assisted in keeping up the ruse, sending tiny little soldiers called Curetes to keep guard outside the cave. Whenever baby Zeus fussed, the Curetes banged their shields and swords together to drown out the noise of his cries.

ULTIMATE REVENGE

Despite his uncommon upbringing, Zeus thrived in the cave and grew to be a great god. Once ready to face the world on his own, he left the comforts of his cave to seek revenge on Cronus by poisoning him. But the poison actually made Cronus so sick to his stomach that he threw up all five of the kids he'd swallowed, plus the rock he mistook for baby Zeus. With a weakened Cronus suddenly up against the six young gods, his reign as the leader of the universe was in jeopardy.

BACK TO THEIR ROOTS

Mythology may be rooted in, well, myth, but some people believe there are signs of this ancient world in real life. In fact, a cave in Crete, Greece, is said to be where Rhea gave birth to Zeus and ultimately hid her son from Cronus. Whether fact or fiction, that doesn't stop thousands of people from checking out these caves to catch a glimpse of where the most famous god may have gotten his start.

MODERN MYTHOLOGY RIGHT ON TIME

For Cronus, timing was everything. The Titan god of time, he oversaw the calendars, seasons, and harvests. In fact, words like "chronology" and "chronicle"—both used to reference time—stem from his legacy. There's also a link between Cronus and Father Time, the fictional figure representing the passage of a new year. Both are depicted in art as older mean wearing robes and carrying a sickle.

CRONUS EVENTUALLY **THREW UP** HIS CHILDREN, AND THEY **CAME OUT** ALIVE.

Titanomachy

ΤΗΣ WAR OF ΤΗΣ TITANS

WHY IT'S WEIRD
This mega sibling squabble took 10 years to hash out.

A DECADE OF DRAMA

Once Cronus coughed up his children, the war was on. On one side: Zeus and the kids Cronus swallowed: Hestia, Demeter, Hera, Hades, and Poseidon. On the other: Cronus and the rest of the Titans. Each side wanted control of the universe, and neither was willing to give up the fight easily. Combine that with the fact that the Titans possessed, well, *titanic* strength, and the war dragged on for a decade.

HELPING HANDS

To boost his side of the battle, Zeus freed the so-called "monsters" that his grandfather, Uranus, had chucked into Tartarus. Yep, those 100-handed (and 50-headed!) giants plus the one-eyed Cyclopes. The story goes that the three giants known as the Hecatoncheires hurled huge boulders at their enemies from mountaintops, one with each hand. That's a lot of rocks!

ARMED AND DANGEROUS

But it was the Cyclopes who should be hailed as the heroes of this war. Master crafters, they created weapons of destruction for three of the gods: A thunderbolt for Zeus, a forked trident for Poseidon, and for Hades, a helmet that made him invisible. With their new weapons in hand, the trio of brothers plotted a plan to overpower the Titans, lock them in Tartarus, and take down Cronus once and for all.

SHOULDERING THE LOAD

The plan worked, and Zeus became ruler of the sky and the king of all gods. Poseidon took over as leader of the Oceans, and Hades was crowned king of the Underworld. As for the other Titans? They were banished to Tartarus, guarded by the Hecatoncheires. Meanwhile, Atlas, the son of the Titan Iapetus and a leader in the battle against the gods, was ordered to hold up the heavens on his shoulders until the end of time. That's one *weighty* punishment.

MODERN MYTHOLOGY
TURN OF PHRASE

The tale of the Titanomachy may be thousands of years old, but its legacy lives on in current times. "Clash of the Titans" is a popular phrase used to describe two major things going up against each other, like a pair of undefeated sports teams heading into a championship game. It's also the title of a blockbuster movie, which borrowed a storyline from mythology to depict the war between gods.

POSEIDON'S **TRIDENT** WAS **SO FORCEFUL** THAT HE COULD **CREATE WAVES TALLER THAN** MOUNTAINS BY SIMPLY **STRIKING THE GROUND** WITH IT.

Zeus

GOD OF THE SKY & HEAVENS

CLAIM TO FAME
He was the ruler of the gods.

WHY HE'S WEIRD Zeus would use lightning bolts to strike down his enemies.

IN THE BEGINNING

Zeus may have gotten a rough start in life—he *was* born in a cave and narrowly escaped being swallowed by his father. But he was in good hooves, err *hands*, with his goat nanny, Amaltheia, and the nymphs who looked after him. Nourished by a diet of goat milk, he grew to be a mighty god with enough smarts and strength to eventually overthrow the Titans to take control of the universe.

IT'S MYTHIC!

Zeus had the ability to turn mortals immortal.

WEATHER MAN

Did a thunderstorm cancel your outdoor birthday party? Blame Zeus! As the god of the sky and thunder, he controlled all of the world's weather, including the wind, the clouds, rain, thunder, and lightning. But Zeus only unleashed the bad stuff as a punishment for someone he believed crossed him. Like the time he hurled a lightning bolt at Ixion, a doctor, after Ixion fell in love with Zeus's wife Hera.

SHAPE-SHIFTER

Zeus was a master of disguise. To trick or confuse people, the cunning king could morph into the shape of an animal, like a bull or a swan. He nabbed his wife Hera by first creating a thunderstorm, then disguising himself as a small cuckoo bird. When she spotted the bird out in the rain, she scooped it up and comforted it. Zeus then switched back into mighty god mode, duping Hera into marriage. Sneaky, sneaky!

MODERN MYTHOLOGY
GOLDEN GOD

Swimmer Michael Phelps may have rightfully earned all 28 of his Olympic medals in the pool, but he can give a little credit to Zeus for all of that bling. After all, without the king of gods, the Olympics may not have even existed. Why? The very first Greek Olympics, held in the city of Olympia in 776 B.C., celebrated and honored Zeus. And those games—featuring events like running, wrestling, and chariot racing—are said to have inspired the modern Olympics, which began in Athens, Greece, in 1896.

ZEUS WAS SAID TO BE **SO STRONG,** HE COULD **SINGLE-HANDEDLY** BEAT A TEAM OF **ALL** OTHER GODS IN TUG-OF-WAR.

Olympus

Even the Greek gods can't escape assigned seats! In Mount Olympus, the Olympian gods gathered on golden thrones in a large courtyard as they ruled over heaven and earth. Here's the seating chart.

HERA
Queen of the gods; Zeus's wife

DEMETER
Goddess of the harvest; Zeus's sister

ARES
God of war; Hera's son

HEPHAESTUS
God of blacksmiths and craftsmen; Zeus's son

APHRODITE
Goddess of love

FIT FOR A KING

Once Zeus was crowned king of the gods, he settled into a towering palace built on top of Mount Olympus—the tallest mountain in Greece—so that the gods could see all of the world below them. Built by the Cyclopes, the palace sparkled with golden floors and gleaming marble accents. Mount Olympus was also home to 11 other Olympian gods and goddesses, all said to have special powers and control over different

WHY IT'S WEIRD

To enter Olympus, you first had to pass through a gate of golden clouds.

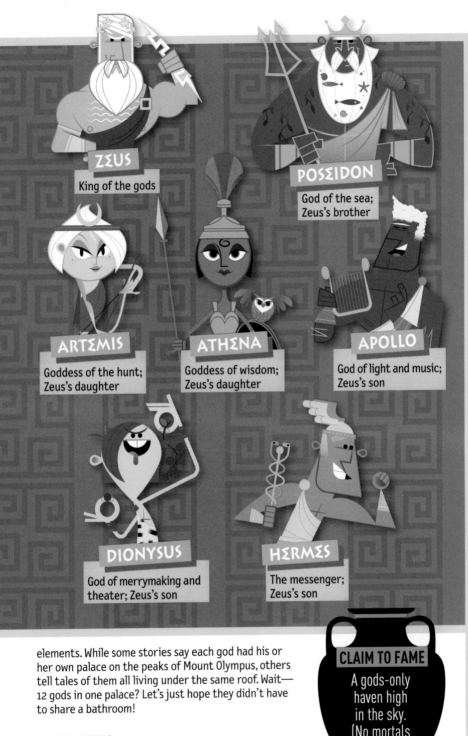

ZEUS

King of the gods

POSEIDON

God of the sea;
Zeus's brother

ARTEMIS

Goddess of the hunt;
Zeus's daughter

ATHENA

Goddess of wisdom;
Zeus's daughter

APOLLO

God of light and music;
Zeus's son

DIONYSUS

God of merrymaking and
theater; Zeus's son

HERMES

The messenger;
Zeus's son

elements. While some stories say each god had his or
her own palace on the peaks of Mount Olympus, others
tell tales of them all living under the same roof. Wait—
12 gods in one palace? Let's just hope they didn't have
to share a bathroom!

EASY LIVING

On Olympus, life was good for the gods. For the most
part, the palace was a peaceful, positive place, with

CLAIM TO FAME

A gods-only
haven high
in the sky.
(No mortals
allowed!)

MODERN MYTHOLOGY
TWIN TOWERS

Greece's Mount Olympus is certainly iconic, but it isn't the only one on Earth. In fact, there's a same-named mountain in Olympia, Washington, U.S.A. So what's the scoop behind the tale of two mountains? When English explorer Captain John Meares went to name the Washington State peak in 1788, he claimed it beautiful enough to "dwell the gods." While both are majestic, Greece's Mount Olympus towers 1,500 feet (457 m) taller than its sister mountain.

plenty of parties and relaxation time. The gods lounged around, eating and drinking. A choir of goddesses known as the Muses and Graces provided endless entertainment, as did Apollo, the god of music, who played songs on a harp-like instrument called a lyre.

That's not to say there wasn't any family drama among the gods. They experienced humanlike emotions including anger and jealousy and they weren't above bickering with their brothers and sisters, either. Gods—they're just like us!

Menu
OF THE
IMMORTALS

When it came to grub, the gods kept it pretty simple! To sustain their immortality, they sipped and munched on just two items.

TO ΣAT: AMBROSIA
A mythical mixture that may have consisted of honey, cheese, olive oil, fruit, and barley

TO DRINK: NΣCTAR
A deliciously sweet drink made from fermented honey

THE CLIFFS SURROUNDING OLYMPUS WERE SAID TO BE SO HIGH AND STEEP THAT NO MORTAL WOULD EVER BE ABLE TO CLIMB THEM.

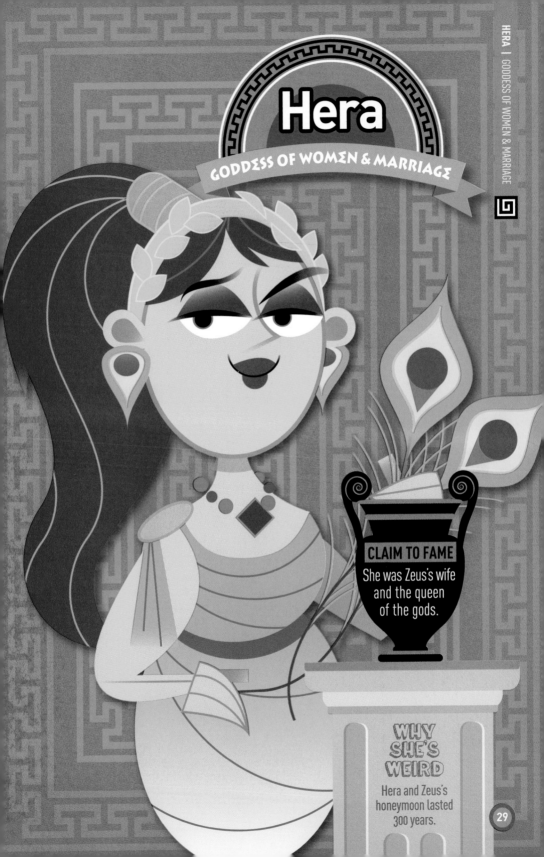

Hera

GODDESS OF WOMEN & MARRIAGE

CLAIM TO FAME
She was Zeus's wife and the queen of the gods.

WHY SHE'S WEIRD
Hera and Zeus's honeymoon lasted 300 years.

MODERN MYTHOLOGY
TALES OF A TAIL

Look closely at a peacock's distinctive tail feathers and you may notice many colorful "eye" markings of blue, gold, green, and red. While these spots are simply a natural feature of the fowl's feathers, the ancient Greeks came up with a story about how they got there. The, um, *tale?* According to myth, Hera had a 100-eyed giant servant named Argus, who met an untimely demise at the hands of Hermes. To honor Argus for all of his service to her, Hera placed each of her 100-eyed servant's peepers on the tail of a peacock, giving the bird its unique spotted feathers.

PROUD AS A PEACOCK

Considered to be the most stunning of all Olympian goddesses, Hera was beautiful—and she knew it. She spent much of her time tending to her personal beauty regimen, like bathing in spring water, slathering herself in fragrant oils, and braiding her long locks. So it's no surprise that Hera is often represented in art alongside a peacock, a bird that proudly shows off its pretty plumage.

FIT TO BE TIED

Zeus had eyes for other women, including mortals, and Hera knew it. To punish him for his bad behavior, she once bound him to his bed with 100 knotted cords and stole his thunderbolt. But the plan backfired when he was freed by one of the Hecatoncheires. Zeus's revenge? Hanging Hera upside down from the sky!

NO WORDS

Hera also sought revenge on other women. Take, for example, a chatty nymph named Echo. When Zeus was having a relationship with another woman, Echo distracted Hera with her nonstop talk so she wouldn't find out about the secret affair. Once she did piece it together, Hera was so livid that she took away Echo's ability to speak. She could only repeat the last few words said to her. Did somebody say *echo ... echo ... echo?*

MOOOOVE OVER

Hera was so clever, not even Zeus could conceal much from her, although he did try. In an attempt to keep one of his mortal wives, Io, a secret, he changed her into a small white cow. Hera saw right through the ruse but pretended not to notice. Instead, she begged Zeus to let her keep the cow. He complied, and Hera then tied her up to a tree and kept her under the careful watch of Argus, a 100-eyed monster. And when Io escaped? Hera ordered a biting fly to constantly sting and chase the cow. Ouch. Lesson learned: Don't mess with Hera!

moooo?

AS THE RULER OF **HEAVEN** AND THE **SKIES,** HERA COULD **CURSE PEOPLE** WITH **BAD STORMS.**

Hestia

GODDESS OF THE HEARTH & HOME

CLAIM TO FAME
She kept the eternal flame on Mount Olympus burning.

WHY SHE'S WEIRD
Hestia was the first kid to be eaten by her father, Cronus, but the last to be thrown up—making her both the oldest and youngest of the siblings.

FIRE AND NICE

Hestia may have lived on Olympus, but she's not often grouped in with the other 12 Olympians. Why not? Myths tell of her offering up her golden throne to the god Dionysus because she was more intent on taking care of the hearth, or the eternal flame inside Mount Olympus. Besides, Hestia was known as a kind, quiet goddess and didn't get involved with the drama often surrounding her siblings. Instead, she kept to herself, never left Olympus, and didn't interfere in the lives of mortals, either. As a result of her minding her own business, Hestia isn't featured in as many myths as her brothers and sisters.

SINGLE LADY

Both the gods Apollo and Poseidon wanted to marry Hestia, but she was set on staying single for life. So she asked Zeus to grant her this wish, and he agreed. Later, he would grant the same wish to Artemis and Athena, and together the trio became known as maiden goddesses—or those who pledged to never marry.

Your house today may look nothing like those that the ancient Greeks dwelled in, but there may be one striking similarity: the fireplace! Back then, the fireplace, or the hearth, was located in the center of the home. They were quite large and used mostly for cooking. While we don't typically cook dinner in our fireplaces today, we do gather around them in the colder months with our families to keep cozy and warm (same goes for bonfires at the beach or huddling around a campfire). And, just like it did in ancient times, the hearth remains a symbol of hospitality and protection at home.

DOMESTIC BLISS

Hestia also had some power to make homes happy—and warm. She wasn't just in charge of keeping Olympus's flames flickering, she was also the protector of hospitality, the preparation of food and bread, and the giver of happiness at home. Later, in ancient Greece, Hestia became a very important figure. The ancient Greeks began and ended each meal with an offering to Hestia, and dedicated the most delicious part of their food to her.

IT'S MYTHIC!

Every city and town in ancient Greece had a public hearth with an eternal flame dedicated to Hestia.

HESTIA IS SAID **TO HAVE HAD OIL** DRIPPING FROM HER **LONG HAIR.**

Poseidon

GOD OF THE SEAS

CLAIM TO FAME
He ruled the seas and could start powerful earthquakes.

WHY HE'S WEIRD
Poseidon rode the waves in a gold chariot pulled by half-horse, half-serpent creatures with golden manes.

WATER WORLD

After the War of the Titans, Poseidon took over the oceans, where he ruled from his undersea palace with his wife, Amphitrite. From there, he controlled the currents, sometimes launching waves giant enough to sink ships. At other times he smoothed the seas to help sailors along. Poseidon's personality was a lot like the sea itself: sometimes rough, sometimes calm and placid. While he was known to be helpful, catch him on a bad day, and he just may flood your land.

NO CONTEST

Although life underwater appeared idyllic, Poseidon wasn't satisfied ruling just the seas. He wanted earthly kingdoms, too, namely the Greek land of Attica. The only problem? Athena, the goddess of wisdom, wanted it, too. So the pair put on a contest. The person who offered up the best gift to the people of the city would win the land. A confident Poseidon stepped up and banged his mighty trident into a rocky hillside, intending to turn it into a flowing spring. The water wasn't fresh, but salty seawater—and undrinkable. Meanwhile, Athena offered the gift that kept on giving: an olive tree. The people of Attica could eat the olives and make olive oil, use the tree's wood, and seek shade beneath its branches. Much to Poseidon's disappointment, Athena not only won the land, but it was renamed after her as well. Ever hear of *Athens*, Greece?

A HORSE, OF COURSE

That's not to say Poseidon didn't make a great impact in the mythological world. Some stories say that he created the horse! Scheming to create the world's most beautiful animal in an attempt to win over the goddess Demeter, Poseidon crafted the animal by smashing his trident into a rock. The ploy to steal Demeter's heart didn't work, but horses became part of Poseidon's persona, and he's often credited with starting the sport of horse racing.

MODERN MYTHOLOGY
POSEIDON IN POP CULTURE

Some might say Poseidon's a regular movie star!

DISNEY'S *THE LITTLE MERMAID*
Ariel's father, King Triton, is loosely based on the sea god, complete with the golden trident.

PIRATES OF THE CARIBBEAN
In *Dead Men Tell No Tales*, the fifth installment in the popular film series, quirky pirate Jack Sparrow is focused on finding the legendary trident of Poseidon to gain control of the seas.

PERCY JACKSON AND THE OLYMPIANS
In this popular book series, the main character, Perseus "Percy" Jackson, is the son of Poseidon and a mortal woman, making him a demigod.

POSEIDON LIVED IN **A PALACE** UNDER THE OCEAN MADE FROM **JEWELS AND CORAL** AND DECORATED WITH **SEA FLOWERS.**

Hades

GOD OF THE UNDERWORLD

CLAIM TO FAME
He oversaw all of the souls of the dead.

WHY HE'S WEIRD He rarely left the Underworld, preferring to stay there instead of on top of Mount Olympus.

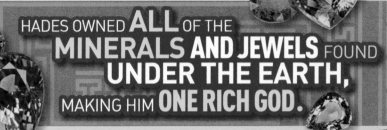

HADES OWNED **ALL** OF THE **MINERALS AND JEWELS** FOUND **UNDER THE EARTH,** MAKING HIM **ONE RICH GOD.**

FEAR NO EVIL

Darkness? Death? Doom and gloom? That kind of scary stuff had *nothing* on Hades. Crowned the overlord of the underground after the Titanomachy, Hades took his new title quite seriously and stayed put in his spooky and dark dwelling. Although he had a place to live on Mount Olympus, he rarely made it up there, preferring to hang out solo in the shadowy spot. There, he oversaw souls of the dead, mostly determining where people wound up after they entered the Underworld.

NOW YOU SEE HIM ...

Move over, Harry Potter. Who needs an invisibility cloak when you've got an invisibility *helmet?* Thanks to the handiwork of the crafty Cyclopes, Hades could hide out wherever he wanted once he popped on his tricky topper. He even let other gods, goddesses, and demigods, like Hermes, Athena, and Perseus, borrow it when they went to battle.

A GOD'S BEST FRIEND

Hades may have been a gloomy god, but he did have somewhat of a soft side. At least for his three-headed dog, Cerberus. When Cerberus wasn't guarding the gate to the Underworld, he'd take rides with Hades across the dark land on a golden chariot. Which makes you wonder: How much did Hades have to feed a dog with three mouths? That's a lot of puppy chow!

MODERN MYTHOLOGY
CURSES!

The ancient Greeks had an odd way of getting back at their enemies: They'd ask the Underworld gods to curse them! Or at least attempt to. Scientists in Athens, Greece, recently discovered 2,400-year-old "curse tablets"—thin sheets made of lead with requests etched into them for specific people to be stuck with bad luck. It's thought that people left these tablets in wells and graves in the hopes that they'd eventually reach the Underworld.

woof!

bark!

ruff!

IT'S MYTHIC!
Hades is the name of both the god and the Underworld itself.

Demeter

GODDESS OF THE HARVEST

CLAIM TO FAME

She taught humans about agriculture and created winter.

WHY SHE'S WEIRD

While searching for her missing daughter, Persephone, she disguised herself as an old lady and claimed to have escaped from pirates.

SNEAK ATTACK

Picture this: A doting mother and her beautiful daughter frolic in a field of flowers. The mom looks on as the girl, fresh and full of life, dances with the grace of a ballerina. This was a day in the idyllic lives of Demeter, who controlled all living things on Earth, and her daughter Persephone. Until Hades stepped on the scene, that is.

Turns out, Hades had fallen in love with Persephone and wanted her to be his queen. But how could a brooding loner from the Underworld woo a delightful being like Persephone? He couldn't—so he kidnapped her! One day as Persephone gathered blooms by a lake, the ground split beneath her feet. Up came Hades, who quickly seized the girl and carted her back to his shadowy kingdom. Persephone was now his queen—and Demeter didn't see a thing.

MODERN MYTHOLOGY
GREAT GRAINS

What does Demeter have to do with that bowl of Cheerios you had for breakfast this morning? Plenty! The word "cereal" comes from Ceres, the Roman name for Demeter. As the goddess of grain, Demeter is credited with the discovery of an ancient strain of wheat, called spelt, and she taught others how to grow and harvest it—and eventually make cereal. So it's fitting that one of the world's favorite ways to start the day is named for this gifted goddess.

AN ENDLESS WINTER

Understandably, Demeter was devastated when her daughter vanished. She searched and searched for her, growing more hopeless by the day. The sadder she became, the more things on Earth began to die: Flowers wilted, trees lost their leaves, and an icy sheath covered the fields. She wound up blaming and cursing the Earth for swallowing Persephone. As animals died and people starved, the gods begged Demeter to return to work. But she just couldn't allow anything to grow while she ached for her daughter.

DEAL MAKER

Things became so barren on Earth that Zeus had to do *something*. He ordered Hades to return Persephone to her mother. But there was a catch: If Persephone ate *anything* while in the Underworld, she would be stuck there for good. But Persephone had accidentally snacked on a few pomegranate seeds during her stay. So a compromise was made: Persephone would spend one month in the Underworld for each seed she swallowed, and the rest of her time with her mother.

'TIS THE SEASONS

From then on, when Demeter and Persephone were together, the Earth burst with life: Flowers bloomed, fields flourished with grains, and the warm sunshine cast its golden glow. But when Persephone returned to her reign as the queen of the Underworld for a few months every year, Demeter grieved. The Earth went back to being icy and barren. And this, the Greeks say, explains how Demeter (with some help from Persephone) created the seasons.

MYTH SAYS THAT WHEN **DEMETER SMILED, PLANTS SPROUTED** AND FRUIT **TREES BLOSSOMED.**

The Underworld

THE KINGDOM OF THE DEAD

DEATH BECOMES THEM

Where did mortals go when they died? According to mythology, every person—no matter whether he or she was good, evil, or in-between—landed in the Underworld. Where they went from there was decided by Hades and a trio of judges—Rhadamanthus, Aeacus, and Minos.

But first, the souls had to get into Hades. Here's how it went down: Once a mortal died, their soul had

SMALL CHANGE

to cross five rivers, representing sorrow, lamentation, fire, forgetfulness, and hate. The soul crossed the river by boat or found another entrance through a cave—either way, it eventually made it to the gates of Hades. There, it met the three-headed dog Cerberus, bearing rows and rows of gnashing, sharp teeth. But he wasn't tasked with keeping the dead out. Rather, he'd attack anyone who tried to leave. Once you were in Hades, there was absolutely no turning back (unless you were lucky enough to be reborn).

CLAIM TO FAME

This was the forever home of all dead mortal souls.

BEFORE AND AFTERLIFE

As king of the Underworld, Hades determined where each soul would call his or her eternal resting place. The Underworld was split into different sections—and where you wound up depended on your behavior on Earth. Here's a basic breakdown.

IF YOU WERE BAD ...
TARTARUS

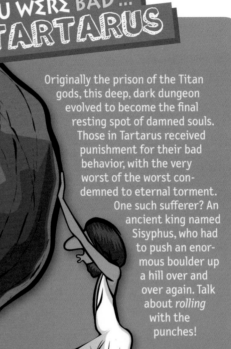

Originally the prison of the Titan gods, this deep, dark dungeon evolved to become the final resting spot of damned souls. Those in Tartarus received punishment for their bad behavior, with the very worst of the worst condemned to eternal torment. One such sufferer? An ancient king named Sisyphus, who had to push an enormous boulder up a hill over and over again. Talk about *rolling* with the punches!

ACCORDING TO MYTH, IT TOOK **NINE DAYS** **AND NINE NIGHTS** TO REACH **THE UNDERWORLD.**

IF YOU WERE GOOD ... ELYSIUM

Exceptionally good or heroic people were sent to Elysium, a blissful, peaceful place of sunshine and warmth. Those lucky enough to land here were given a choice whether they wanted to stay put, or be reborn after 1,000 years and placed back on Earth as a brand-new baby. If you were reborn three times and went on to return to Elysium after each stint, you'd get a one-way ticket to paradise. Not bad!

IN THE MIDDLE ... ASPHODEL FIELDS

IT'S MYTHIC!

Anyone who landed in the Asphodel Fields had to drink from the river of forgetfulness, wiping away all memories of life on Earth.

So let's say you didn't do anything saintly or brilliant during your time on Earth. But you didn't commit any crimes, either. Those stuck in the middle between good and evil were guided to Asphodel Fields. Here, the dead became shadowy versions of their earthly selves and wandered around aimlessly, leading an average existence not too much different than their lives on Earth.

MODERN MYTHOLOGY ANCIENT PASSAGE

Be careful where you're walking while in Pamukkale, Turkey—you may just slide down to the gates of Hades! A team of scientists from an Italian university recently discovered a large opening among the ruins of the ancient city of Hierapolis, founded around 190 B.C. This "gate"—also known as a Ploutonion—is believed to be a place where residents used to make sacrifices to the god of the Underworld.

Hermes

CLAIM TO FAME

He passed along important messages between gods and mortals.

WHY HE'S WEIRD

He created the first lyre, an instrument similar to a harp, out of a tortoise's shell, using stretched-out sheep guts for the strings.

NOT SO INNOCENT

Hermes was the son of Zeus and Maia, a beautiful nymph and daughter of the Titan Atlas. Born in a deep, dark cave hidden away from Zeus's wrathful wife, Hera, Hermes displayed dazzling wit from the time he was born. As a newborn, he snuck out of his cave and found a tortoise. And what was a brilliant, resourceful baby to do with such a creature? Why, make a musical instrument out of it of course! He is also credited with inventing fire.

tee hee hee

Hermes was also mischievous. As a baby, he once stole Apollo's cattle, sneakily leading them back to his cave. When Apollo found out about the stolen cows, he threatened to toss Hermes into Tartarus. Until, that is, Hermes began playing a song on his new lyre. Apollo became enchanted by the beautiful music and ultimately forgave him—especially after Hermes promised to give him the instrument and teach him to play. Because how could you *ever* stay mad at a sweet, lyre-playing baby?

GET THE MESSAGE

An impressed Zeus took note of Hermes' many talents early on and soon selected him to be his very own messenger. Whenever Zeus needed something retrieved or an errand run, he'd call up his speedy son to do the job. This included fetching Persephone from the clutches of Hades, delivering orders, and passing along messages between the gods and mortals. He also led dead souls down to the Underworld from Earth. Phew! You can't say Hermes wasn't a hard worker!

AS A BRAND-**NEW BABY,** HERMES COULD **ALREADY CRAWL AND TALK.**

HOW TO BΣ HERMES

Not just any god had the tools to be the quickest, wittiest god in the land. Here are the items that helped Hermes get around:

- **GOLDEN-WINGED HAT:** With the ability to fly, Hermes could move between the worlds of the gods, humans, and the dead.
- **WINGED SANDALS:** These snazzy shoes gave Hermes super speed to carry messages.
- **CAPE:** Hermes always kept his cape on to be ready to travel at a moment's notice.
- **STAFF:** Also called a caduceus, this magical stick with snakes wrapped around it could control and heal mortals.

Athena

GODDESS OF WAR, WISDOM & THE ARTS

CLAIM TO FAME
She was the namesake of Athens, Greece.

WHY SHE'S WEIRD
She had the power to turn her enemies into icky things like spiders and snakes.

BRAIN CHILD

Athena sprang to life in the weirdest way: from Zeus's forehead! The story goes that Zeus swallowed Athena's mother, Metis, while she was pregnant with the future goddess. A few months later, he came down with a horrible headache. So he had his blacksmith split his head open with an ax—and out popped Athena, ready for action! She wasted no time making a name—and a home—for herself on Mount Olympus. She shared her wisdom with both her fellow gods and mortals alike.

so sss-cary!

STONE COLD

Athena had special powers—and she wasn't afraid to use them. Especially when it came to teaching someone a lesson. Take the tale of Medusa, for example. A beautiful young girl with a mega-size ego, Medusa often bragged that she was the fairest maiden in all the land. Once Athena caught wind of her boastful claims, she did what any wise goddess would do: She turned Medusa into a monster, transforming her long, golden locks into a nest of hissing snakes. The curse made Medusa so scary that the mere sight of her could turn someone to stone—and she was banished to the far ends of the Earth. Well, *that'll* teach her!

ALONG CAME A SPIDER

One thing's for sure: Athena was always up for a challenge (see page 35 to read about her matchup against Poseidon). So when a mortal woman named Arachne tossed the idea of a weaving contest her way, she couldn't turn it down. The thing is, Arachne's finished product portrayed Zeus in a negative light—and Athena wasn't happy about it. Athena destroyed Arachne's work and then used a potion to shrivel her into oblivion. Then Athena took pity on Arachne and brought her back to life as a spider—and Arachne and her descendants have been weavers that hang from threads ever since.

MODERN MYTHOLOGY
CRAWL ON

Scientists in France recently borrowed from Greek mythology to name a newly discovered spider fossil that dates back some 305 million years. The fossil is from one of the world's earliest known spiders and is named *Idmonarachne brasieri*, a reference to Idmon, the father of the skilled weaver Arachne. The word "arachnid" itself is tied to Arachne as well—referring to invertebrates that have four pairs of legs and no wings or antennae, including spiders, scorpions, mites, and ticks.

ATHENA WAS **BORN FULLY GROWN** AND **WEARING ARMOR.**

IT'S MYTHIC!

Athena was famous for her majestic gray eyes. She was also the patron of craftsmen and taught the Greeks how to cook and sew.

Artemis

GODDESS OF THE HUNT

CLAIM TO FAME
She was the strong, independent ruler of the woods.

WHY SHE'S WEIRD Artemis spent her time frolicking in the forest, hunting with invisible arrows.

ON THE HUNT

Imagine being born with such smarts and strength that you could help deliver a baby mere moments after taking your first breath of life. That's how Artemis is described: Popping out as a tiny infant only to turn around and help her mother, the Titan Leto, deliver her twin brother, Apollo. As Artemis grew, so did her skills and savvy. She became an amazingly accurate hunter with perfect aim, spending her days in the mountains with her loyal hounds and nymphs.

MODERN MYTHOLOGY
STORY BEHIND THE STARS

When the night sky is filled with stars, one of the easiest constellations to spot is Orion—a collection of stars that make up his club, lion's skin, belt, and sword. The story goes that Orion, a loyal hunting partner and friend of Artemis, was placed among the stars by the goddess after she accidentally shot and killed him (some stories say her twin brother, Apollo, tricked her into shooting him). Distraught by his death, Artemis made a home for him in the sky, alongside his hunting dogs, Canis Major and Canis Minor. Today, Orion remains as one of the brightest and most recognizable constellations in the sky.

HARSH LESSON

Don't mess with their mama! After hearing a mortal queen named Niobe brag about being better than Leto because she had more children, Artemis and Apollo took action. As a punishment for her pride, they killed *all* 14 of Niobe's kids. Harsh? Yes. But this tale is often used to highlight just how far the gods would go to defend their loyalty—and to teach humans about being humble.

AS YOU WISH...

Zeus had many children, but he especially doted on his daughter Artemis. As a toddler, he told her he'd give her anything in the world. Here's her wish list.

MY WISH LIST
- To stay single forever and never marry
- A bow and arrow
- A tunic to wear while hunting
- 60 nymphs to be friends and hunting partners
- All the mountains in the world

A **TEMPLE** DEDICATED TO ARTEMIS IN **TURKEY** IS ONE OF THE **SEVEN WONDERS** OF THE **ANCIENT** WORLD.

Apollo

GOD OF THE ARTS, MUSIC, HEALING & LIGHT

CLAIM TO FAME

After teaching men the art of medicine, Apollo became known as "the Healer."

WHY HE'S WEIRD

Apollo would disguise himself as a dolphin to help sailors at sea.

SLAYING THE SERPENT

Apollo didn't waste much time getting to work as a god. At just four days old, Apollo set out to slay the giant serpent named Python who had been slithering around the mountain town of Delphi—then thought to be the center of the Earth—destroying crops, polluting streams, and scaring everyone around it. Armed with magical arrows, Apollo hunted down Python—said to be as big as a hillside—and killed it with 1,000 poisonous arrows. Not bad for a baby!

IN TUNE

Remember when tiny Hermes gave Apollo his homemade lyre? That exchange led to Apollo's love for music. He rarely went anywhere without his instrument—he even played a victory song when he slayed the serpent. And, alongside the nine Muses (goddesses said to inspire music and art), he led all of the entertainment on Olympus. Apollo eventually passed this musical gift down to Orpheus, his son with the Muse Calliope. It's said that when Orpheus played the lyre and sang, nothing on Earth could resist the power of his music.

APOLLO GREW TO BE A FULL-SIZE GOD IN ONE DAY.

FATHER-SON FEUD

Apollo was quite the can-do kind of god. But there was one thing he couldn't master: getting along with his dad, Zeus. Their beef began when Zeus caught on that Apollo's son Asclepius could resurrect the dead. Zeus didn't like that Asclepius's actions were upsetting his brother Hades, who wanted more dead souls in the Underworld. So Zeus killed Asclepius by striking him with his thunderbolt. Apollo retaliated by killing the Cyclopes—the creatures who created Zeus's deadly weapons—and was temporarily banished from Olympus by Zeus. How'd he spend those days? By herding cattle for a mortal king. At least the punishment only lasted a year!

IT'S MYTHIC!

The Greeks believed the sun was pulled across the sky by Apollo's chariot, led by golden horses.

MODERN MYTHOLOGY
MARK OF A CHAMPION

In artwork, Apollo is usually shown with a wreath of interlocking branches and dark laurel leaves around his head. This represents his unrequited love for a nymph named Daphne who was transformed into a laurel tree by the river god Peneus while trying to escape Apollo's advances. While Apollo may have been unlucky in love, he wasn't in sports! So, in a nod to Apollo's athleticism, athletes in ancient times began receiving crowns similar to the god's for winning a race or event. Today, that tradition continues, with winners sporting laurel crowns at the modern Olympics and at major events like the New York City Marathon.

Hephaestus

GOD OF FIRE & CRAFTSMEN

CLAIM TO FAME
The blacksmith of Olympus

FALLING SHORT

Compared to his fellow flawless gods and goddesses, Hephaestus stood out. He had a limp and other physical imperfections—traits that his shallow and vain mother, Hera, couldn't handle. She despised him so much that she tossed him off Olympus. He fell for many days before landing in the ocean near an island. A pair of sea goddesses rescued him and brought him back to their underwater cave. With their loving care, Hephaestus grew up to be a kind, helpful, handy, and hardworking god.

SO CRAFTY

Later, when Zeus recognized Hephaestus's knack for craftsmanship, he allowed him back on Olympus. As the god of fire, Hephaestus spent his time toiling away in his

hee-haw

HEPHAESTUS RODE **AROUND** IN A **DONKEY CART** INSTEAD OF A **CHARIOT.**

workshop crafting goods out of metal, stone, gold, silver, and bronze. There wasn't anything Hephaestus couldn't make. He even crafted his own handmaidens out of gold to help lighten his load!

LOCKED UP

For the most part, Hephaestus was an upbeat, helpful god. When it came to Hera, however, he just couldn't be jolly. Hephaestus wanted revenge for her rejecting him at birth. So he whipped up a golden throne, offering it to Hera as a gift. This was no ordinary throne, though; invisible chains locked Hera to the chair, so when she tried to get up, she couldn't move.

If it were up to Hephaestus, Hera would stay stuck in that throne for all eternity. But the other gods wanted her out and encouraged Hephaestus to free her. He finally agreed to let her go, but on the condition that she'd arrange a marriage between him and the beautiful goddess Aphrodite. Hera agreed, and the unlikely pair married. (More about them in the next chapter!)

MODERN MYTHOLOGY
HOT HOME

We now know that a complex mix of factors, including a buildup of magma beneath the Earth's crust, causes volcanic eruptions. But back in the day, folks had different theories. In fact, many ancient Greeks blamed Hephaestus! The story goes that Hephaestus's hangout was located beneath a volcano—a fitting place for the fire god (the Romans actually called him Vulcan, which is where we get the word "volcano"). And every time he created something new in his fiery workshop, he'd set off another eruption.

Today, Hephaestus is still associated with Mount Etna, on the island of Sicily in Italy. Europe's highest active volcano at 10,922 feet (3,329 m). And given how hard Hephaestus worked, it's no surprise there is still almost daily activity on Etna!

HΣPHAΣSTUS'S HANDIWORK

Hephaestus made many useful things for the gods. Here's a collection of some of his creations.

- **PANDORA:** The first mortal woman in the world, made out of clay
- **GOLDEN CHARIOT:** For the sun god Apollo to ride across the sky
- **WINGED HAT AND WINGED SANDALS:** These gave the messenger god Hermes extra speed and the ability to fly.
- **SILVER BOW WITH SILVER ARROWS:** Eros used these to pierce the hearts of mortals and gods, forcing them to fall in love.
- **ARMOR AND WEAPONS:** He worked with a one-eyed Cyclops to create golden shields for Greek heroes like Heracles, Athena, and Achilles, as well as thunderbolts for Zeus.
- **HOMES AND THRONES:** Aside from all of the palaces on Mount Olympus, he built the gods' thrones, too.

Aphrodite

GODDESS OF LOVE & BEAUTY

CLAIM TO FAME
The fairest goddess
of all

WHY SHE'S WEIRD
Aphrodite used
a swan-drawn
cart to glide
through the air.

A SPLASHY START

With gorgeous looks and divine charm, there wasn't much not to, um, love about Aphrodite. Even the way she entered the world was graceful. According to the story, a single drop of Uranus's blood fell down from Olympus into the sea, creating the stunning goddess. She emerged from the sea foam fully grown, riding to shore in a clam shell. As she walked upon the land, fields of flowers bloomed beneath her feet. Well *that's* one way to make a first impression!

IMPERFECT UNION

Aphrodite could've had her pick of husbands. After all, the mere sight of her made both mortals and gods fall head over heels in love with her. But when it came to pinning her down, the fire god Hephaestus was the most persistent. He trapped his mother, Hera, in a golden throne until she agreed to arrange a marriage between the two of them. Aphrodite wanted nothing to do with the not-so-handsome Hephaestus, but she couldn't argue with the queen. And so began another unhappily-ever-after mythological marriage.

LESS THAN LOYAL

Hephaestus may have put a ring on it, but Aphrodite was less than loyal. She sought out love with other gods, including Ares, the god of war (more on him on page 59), and Hermes, as well as with mortals. Hephaestus knew about these affairs and even tried to embarrass her for her dishonesty, but no one could stay angry at Aphrodite for too long. In the end, Hephaestus couldn't do much about Aphrodite's actions. She wound up having a son, Eros, some say with Ares. Together, Aphrodite and Eros were in charge of making people and gods fall in love.

IT'S MYTHIC!
The Greek word for foam, as in sea foam, is *aphros*—a likely nod to Aphrodite.

isn't she lovely?

SOME ANCIENT GREEKS WERE SAID TO **FALL IN LOVE** WITH **STATUES** OF **APHRODITE.**

"VENUS DE MILO"

LOVE AND WAR

Aphrodite was all about love—but she may have had a hand in starting the Trojan War! Although experts aren't sure if the war was a real battle or not, myth says that it all began when Zeus asked Trojan prince Paris to select the most beautiful goddess among Aphrodite, Athena, and Hera. The winner would receive a golden apple. Each goddess was as gorgeous as the other, and Paris had trouble picking the prettiest. So Athena promised him strength and invincibility, Hera offered to make him the ruler of the world. And Aphrodite said she'd give him the most beautiful mortal woman on the planet. Paris couldn't resist the temptation tossed his way from Aphrodite and gave her the apple.

In turn, Aphrodite gave Paris Helen of Troy, the queen of Sparta. Only problem? She was already married! Her husband, King Menelaus, grew understandably angry when Paris stole her away. He declared war on Troy—an epic battle that lasted 10 years and cost the lives of thousands.

MODERN MYTHOLOGY
UP IN ARMS

Aphrodite inspired love among all around her. And, for some, she sparked creativity, too. In fact, the "Venus de Milo"—one of the most famous sculptures in the world—is believed to represent the goddess of love (Venus is the Roman name for the goddess). Discovered in a pile of rubble among ruins on the Greek island of Milos, the six-foot-eight-inch (2-m) marble statue is said to have been produced by an artist named Alexandros of Antioch around 100 B.C.

While the sculpture is stunning, it's not quite complete: Venus is famously missing her arms. Experts say that the limbs likely broke off over time. But that doesn't stop thousands of people from visiting Venus at her home in the Louvre Museum in Paris, France, every day.

Eros
GOD OF LOVE

CLAIM TO FAME
He made people fall in love by shooting arrows at them.

STRAIGHT TO THE HEART

Armed with magical, golden arrows, Eros could make anyone fall in love. He'd simply shoot an arrow into the heart of unsuspecting gods and mortals and boom: They'd fall head over heels with the first person they saw—whether they wanted to or not.

While Eros's special powers are well defined, his origins are a bit murkier. Some stories say he's Aphrodite's son with Ares, while others claim Zeus to be his father. Other tales tell of him being the son of Gaea, making him as old as the Earth. Either way, he wound up as Aphrodite's constant companion, and the two of them would work together to spread love all over the land.

WHY HE'S WEIRD
In art, Eros is shown as either a baby or a young man.

57

MODERN MYTHOLOGY
CALLING CUPID

Just call him baby face! In many works of ancient art, Eros is shown as a chubby infant with a set of wide, white wings, carrying a quiver of arrows and a bow. Sound familiar? This depiction is likely where our modern version of Cupid comes from. Although Eros is described in very early works of art as a handsome teenager, through the years, his image eventually evolved to the sweet, cherubic Cupid who makes his annual appearance every February.

SHOT THROUGH THE HEART AND EROS TO BLAME.

ARROW MINDED

A dutiful sidekick, Eros did pretty much whatever Aphrodite asked. Especially when she promised him a sweet reward for his task! One day, Aphrodite offered her son a toy—a golden ball that released a trail of flames once it was tossed—to pierce the heart of Medea, the mortal daughter of a famous king. Aphrodite wanted Medea to fall in love with Greek hero Jason so she could use her powers as a sorceress to help him in taking the Golden Fleece, a coveted trophy. Eager for the toy, Eros shot Medea with an arrow. She became instantly smitten with Jason—and helped him grab the fleece.

Sometimes, Aphrodite's acts backfired on her. She ordered Eros to shoot an arrow at the gorgeous mortal princess Psyche. Aphrodite was jealous of Psyche's beauty and wanted her to fall in love with the ugliest man on Earth. Little did she know that Eros would accidentally shoot himself with an arrow and become enamored by the princess himself. He pursued Psyche, ultimately marrying her and making her a goddess.

bull's-eye!

IT'S MYTHIC! The Roman name for Eros is Cupid.

EROS USED OWL OR DOVE FEATHERS TO HELP HIS ARROWS FLY.

Ares

GOD OF WAR

CLAIM TO FAME
He started many battles and wars.

WHY HE'S WEIRD He preferred to dress in battle armor even if he wasn't fighting.

STIR IT UP

He symbolized war. He loved to fight. And he counted folks like Pain, Panic, Famine, and Oblivion among his best friends. So it's no wonder Ares wasn't the most popular of the gods. When he came around, senseless war, brutality, and bloodshed soon followed. Even his father, Zeus, wasn't a fan of Ares' aggression and violent ways. Unable to resist a conflict, when the ancient Greeks went to war, Ares often got involved.

SNEAKY SIDEKICK

Ares hardly went anywhere without his trusty buddy Eris, the spirit of disagreement. She'd stir up trouble and then let Ares swoop in when things escalated from trash-talk to actual fighting. Once, she showed up uninvited to a wedding with a gleaming golden apple that was to go to the most beautiful goddess. When she tossed it into the crowd of guests, chaos broke out as Hera, Aphrodite, and Athena fought for the shiny prize. Trojan prince Paris was tasked with selecting the fairest of them all, and the goddess of love eventually earned the trophy.

IT'S MYTHIC!
Ares' constant companion? His sister Eris, the goddess of chaos.

yoo-hoo, ladies!

Bloodshed might as well have been Ares' middle name. Responsible for countless—and point-less—battles, Ares is always associated with the red stuff. So it's not a shocker that the red planet—aka Mars, which is what the Romans called him—is named after the god of war. The ancient Romans gave the title to the planet, which actually gets its color from oxi-dized iron, in the same chemical reaction that turns blood red. Ares' sons Phobos ("fear") and Deimos ("flight") are also immortalized in space, serving as the namesakes for Mars's two lumpy, crater-pocked moons.

WHAT A PAIN!

Ares may have had plenty of experience in battle, but he was not a skilled soldier. And when it came to pain? Forget about it! Ares would scream so loudly when injured that his cries could be heard for miles. Seeking sympathy from his father, he'd always run back to Olympus, where Zeus would bandage him up and treat his wounds with the ointment of the gods. But Zeus had little sympathy for his son, even calling him the worst and most hateful of all of his children. And considering the king of the gods had nearly 100 kids, that's a super low blow.

LOVE AND WAR

Ares did have a couple of good qualities, though. Tall and hand-some, he caught the eye of many goddesses and mortals, includ-ing none other than Aphrodite. The thing is, Aphrodite was married to Hephaestus—who grew very angry when he found out about the secret fling. So he crafted an invisible net to catch Ares and Aphrodite in an embrace. Hephaestus then invited all of the gods to check out and laugh at the humiliated, entrapped couple. Hephaestus: 1, Ares: 0.

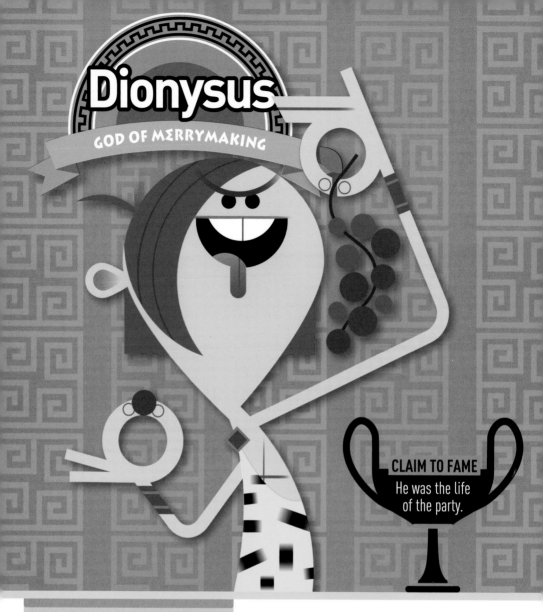

Dionysus

GOD OF MERRYMAKING

CLAIM TO FAME
He was the life of the party.

WHY HE'S WEIRD

He was born from Zeus's thigh.

A TALE OF TWO BIRTHS

The youngest of all of the Olympians, Dionysus was the only one of the 12 great gods whose mother, Semele, was a mortal. And how he came into this world is just as unique. Some say that he was born first to his mother, who died in a fire after being struck by Zeus's thunderbolt. Zeus rescued the tiny baby from the ashes and then quickly sewed him into his thigh to protect the baby until he was ready to be born. After a few months, Zeus gave birth to the baby god, whose name means "child of the double door," reflecting his two-part entry.

RAISED BY NYMPHS

Eager to hide the tiny Dionysus from his jealous wife, Hera, Zeus had Hermes carry him to a faraway valley where he was tended to by a crew of nymphs. There, he had an idyllic upbringing, making friends with leopards and tigers, and ultimately inventing wine out of the bunches of grapes that grew in his valley. Dionysus became famous for this skill, traveling from island to island in a flowing purple robe to teach others the art of winemaking, bringing fun wherever he wandered.

SEE YA, PIRATES

Handsome and regal looking with his long jet black hair and a crown of ivy, Dionysus was once mistaken for a prince by a crew of greedy pirates who wanted to hold him at ransom. Dionysus pleaded with the pirates, trying to convince them that he was neither a prince nor rich. But the pirates didn't believe him, and kept him trapped on their ship. But here's the thing: Dionysus had the power to create wine out of *anything*, including the ocean—and he could shape-shift, too. So when he forced vines to sprout out of the sea, made wine rain down from the sky, and turned himself into a ferocious lion, the baffled pirates jumped overboard. Instead of letting them drown, Dionysus used his powers to turn them into dolphins. Now *that's* a good god!

IN THE STARS

Dionysus may not have been a prince, but he did have royal taste when it came to love. He fell for Ariadne, the mortal princess of Crete, after finding her stranded and alone on the island of Naxos. The pair went on to have a very happy marriage, but unlike her husband, Ariadne could not live forever. When she died, Dionysus dedicated stars in the heavens in her honor. Today, the constellation Corona Borealis—a semicircle arc of stars also known as the northern crown—is said to represent the jewel-studded crown given to Ariadne by Dionysus.

IT'S MYTHIC!

It was once illegal in some parts of Rome to worship the god of merrymaking.

MODERN MYTHOLOGY
SINGING THEIR TUNE

The love story between Dionysus and Ariadne was so epic, it inspired a famous opera. *Ariadne auf Naxos* made its debut in 1912 and is still performed around the world. The opera—sung entirely in German—tells the tale of a lovelorn princess who believes her fate is sealed when her first husband takes off to Athens without her. That is, until, the dashing Dionysus stumbles onto the shores of her island and sweeps her off her feet—and up to the heavens.

DIONYSUS RAISED HIS MOTHER FROM THE DEAD AND BROUGHT HER TO MOUNT OLYMPUS.

Pan

GOD OF NATURE & RUSTIC MUSIC

CLAIM TO FAME
He invented the pan flute out of reeds.

WHY HE'S WEIRD
Pan had the upper body of a man but the legs of a goat and two horns coming out of his head.

THE NAME PAN—MEANING "ALL"—
REFERS TO THIS GOD'S ABILITY TO
CHARM EVERYONE HE MET.

GOAT BOY

Born to Hermes and a wood nymph in a beautiful green valley, Pan wasn't your typical bouncing baby boy. He emerged giggling and bleating, with the features of a goat: a pair of horns sprouting from his forehead, a beard, pointed ears, and hooves instead of feet. His mother took one look at him and bolted. But Hermes had nothing but love for his son, and brought him to Mount Olympus. There, Pan impressed the gods with his sweet and happy-go-lucky personality. They delighted in his dancing, singing, music-playing ways, and soon the young god became one of the most popular figures on Olympus.

SCARED YA!

When not entertaining his fans, Pan could be found frolicking through the forest. And though fun-loving and joyful, Pan had a sneaky side. The story goes that he'd hide out in the bushes and rustle branches as a traveler passed by. As the traveler picked up his pace, Pan would scurry ahead through the forest and rustle more leaves and let out a high-pitched bleat, then watch in excitement as the traveler grew more fearful, picking up the pace in anticipation of being chased by a wild animal. That sudden, uncontrollable, heart-pounding terror he incited can also be described as *pan*-ic. Get it?

LOST LOVE

One day, while wandering in the woods, Pan locked eyes on a beautiful nymph named Syrinx. Though he was smitten, Syrinx was scared of the half goat, half man. She called upon the gods to rescue her from being captured. And the gods answered, turning her into water reeds sticking up out of a nearby river. When Pan went to approach Syrinx, all he found were the hollow sticks waving in the water. Disappointed but determined to honor his love, he cut the reeds to different lengths, sealed them with wax, and made the Syrinx: a flute named after the girl who got away.

MODERN MYTHOLOGY
LOST BOYS UNITE!

Did the myth of Pan spark one of the most famous storybook characters of all time? Never (never) say never! Some experts have drawn comparisons between the Greek god and Peter Pan. Besides the fact that Peter played the pan flute, he was also described by *Peter Pan* author J. M. Barrie as "betwixt-and-between," a boy who can fly and speak the language of birds—a definite comparison to his half-goat, half-boy namesake. Plus, both Pan and Peter Pan both hail from mythical, magical places known for lush, green meadows and soaring waterfalls. One main difference? While Peter Pan is famously known to fly, Pan definitely kept his hooves firmly on the ground.

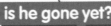
is he gone yet?

IT'S MYTHIC!
Shepherds often left pricey possessions, like vases and lamps, in caves as gifts to Pan.

Titans 2.0

THE SECOND GENERATION OF GIANTS

Don't mess with these descendants! The children of Uranus and Gaea's superpowered six-pack of kids—also known as the Titans—produced a second round of giants who were just as powerful as their parents. Like their parents, these awesome offspring are also known as Titans, and they each have special roles and responsibilities of their own. Here are some of the standouts among this supersize squad.

IT'S MYTHIC!

Aside from Metis, Tethys and Oceanus had some 3,000 daughters, known as the Oceanids, who watched over lakes, ponds, and streams.

OCEANUS — **TETHYS**

METIS
Goddess of wisdom

CLYMENE — **IAPETUS**

PROMETHEUS
God of creation (man)

ATLAS
God of strength

EPIMETHEUS
God of creation (animals)

MENOETIUS
God of violence and anger

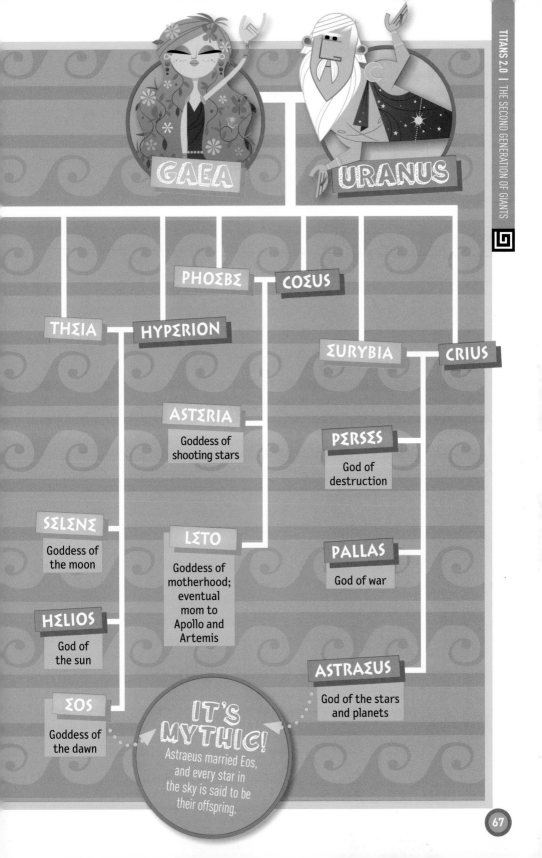

GAEA

URANUS

PHOEBE

COEUS

THEIA

HYPERION

EURYBIA

CRIUS

ASTERIA

Goddess of
shooting stars

PERSES

God of
destruction

SELENE

Goddess of
the moon

LETO

Goddess of
motherhood;
eventual
mom to
Apollo and
Artemis

PALLAS

God of war

HELIOS

God of
the sun

ASTRAEUS

God of the stars
and planets

EOS

Goddess of
the dawn

IT'S
MYTHIC!
Astraeus married Eos,
and every star in
the sky is said to be
their offspring.

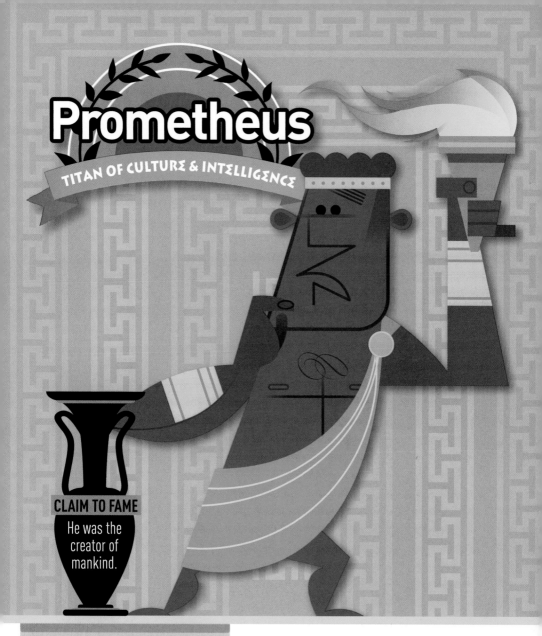

Prometheus

TITAN OF CULTURE & INTELLIGENCE

CLAIM TO FAME
He was the creator of mankind.

WHY HE'S WEIRD
He made mortals out of clay and water.

HEY, MAN

In the beginning, the gods on Mount Olympus seemed to have everything they could ever imagine wanting: a beautiful home overlooking all of the land and sea, golden thrones, endless buffets of fabulous feasts, and music and dancing around the clock. But Prometheus—known for his spot-on foresight—wanted more. He wanted to make the world smarter and better than ever. So, as one theory goes, he came up with the idea to create a race of helpful humans out of clay.

And how does one make a man, you might ask? Prometheus simply took clay from the Earth, mixed it with water and some of his own tears, and formed figures. Each figure had two legs so it could walk upright and gaze up at the stars—and, of course, at Mount Olympus.

MAN'S BEST FRIEND

Prometheus was proud of the people he produced. It's said he invented intelligence just so that he could give it to the human race. Prometheus also looked after them by bringing them the gift of fire and teaching them how to cook and make tools out of the hot flame. Some stories say he also taught humans how to sew, and educated them on subjects like astronomy, medicine, navigation, metalworking, architecture, and writing. Pretty soon, humans were independent and capable, a fact that upset Zeus. He didn't like how humans weren't as reliant on the gods as they once were—and decided to do something about it.

FIRED UP

Prometheus lived to help humans—even if it meant defying Zeus in the process. Once, Zeus withheld fire from humankind, fearing they would use this "technology" for evil. As a result, humans grew miserable and cold, helpless without metal tools and forced to eat raw meat. Concerned about humans' ability to survive, Prometheus stole fire from the gods and brought it down to mankind. When Zeus looked down and saw humans warming themselves by a campfire, he became irate. As punishment, he had Prometheus chained to a rock, where a giant eagle would peck out his liver every day. Because he was immortal, Prometheus's liver grew back every night, prompting the bird to return daily to peck away until the hero Heracles finally set him free.

more liver!

IT'S MYTHIC!

There's a gilded statue of Prometheus at New York City's Rockefeller Center.

MODERN MYTHOLOGY
ETERNAL FLAME

One of the most anticipated events of the Olympic Games? The torch relay, in which people pass the famous Olympic torch from place to place until it reaches the host city of the Games. And we can thank Prometheus for this tradition, as the torch's flame is meant to represent the fire he gave to humankind. Prometheus is also thought to have been integral to inspiring the relay itself, as it's a throwback to ancient Greece when runners would participate in races known as *lampadedromia*. In the race—which celebrated gods including Prometheus—a runner held a torch in their hand and passed it on to the next runner. The first team to reach the finish line with the torch still lit won. That must've been some *hot* competition!

PROMETHEUS AND HIS **TWIN BROTHER,** EPIMETHEUS, ARE CREDITED WITH **CREATING ALL** OF THE **WORLD'S** ANIMALS.

5 Ages of Man
THE HISTORY OF HUMANKIND

How has the human race evolved and changed from the beginning of time? Based on the writings of a famous ancient poet named Hesiod, Greek mythology breaks down the creation of humankind through a series of five eras, or ages.

THE GOLDEN AGE

THE MOOD: Happy and peaceful

During the Golden Age, spring lasted forever and people were said to age backward.

War? What's that? During the Golden Age, life was completely peaceful, without any conflict. With the Titan Cronus ruling over all the land, gods and humans lived harmoniously together. Trees were forever ripe with fruit, fields were rich with grain, and flowers bloomed in beautiful colors. No one had to work, and this stress-free lifestyle meant mortals lived long and happy lives. And when they died? They passed away painlessly as though they were simply drifting off into a dream before turning into spirits who kept watch over all of the Earth.

THE SILVER AGE

THE MOOD: Playful and foolish

After all of the folks from the Golden Age died, Zeus—the new ruler of the world—replaced them with another set of mortals. Just like in the Golden Age, mortals in the Silver Age lived together peacefully ... for about 100 years. Then things got weird: Each human would stay a kid for 100 years before growing up to adulthood at the very end of their lives. The grown-ups of the Silver Age were weak, sick, and did not get along. Zeus also found them disrespectful of the gods, so he wound up tossing them all in Tartarus. There, they'd wander around aimlessly as spirits of the Underworld.

In the Silver Age, Zeus shortened spring so that humans would have to learn to build shelter for the winter.

THE BRONZE AGE

THE MOOD: Conflicted and violent

This generation of men lived in homes made out of bronze and ate the hearts of fellow men instead of bread.

After the failure of the Silver Age, Zeus wanted a do-over. So Zeus had Prometheus mold another generation of mortals out of clay. Unlike the humans of the Silver Age, these men were tough, trained warriors. Zeus armed them with bronze weapons, which they eventually used against each other in war. The world, once filled with peace and tranquility, was now corrupt with battles and bloodshed. Their violent ways continued until they ultimately destroyed each other, landing in the Underworld for all eternity.

THE HEROIC AGE

THE MOOD: Spirited and courageous

Hello, heroes! During this time, demigods, mortals who were related to the gods and had special qualities, like Heracles and Achilles, arrived. These noble warriors braved major battles, including the Trojan War, where many of them died on the battlefield. They then went to a part of the Underworld known as the Elysium, to exist forevermore in a happy, tranquil afterlife. During this time, Zeus released his father, Cronus, from his prison in Tartarus and made him ruler of the Elysium.

Heroes—mortals who performed superhuman acts—were rewarded with a happily ever after(life).

THE IRON AGE

THE MOOD: Somber and dark

During the Iron Age, it's said that babies were born with gray hair.

Zeus created this fifth—and final—age of men, and along with them came every kind of hardship. Mortals toiled away at endless jobs, growing more bitter and angry as each day passed. Constantly conflicted and overwhelmed with stress, humans grew old quickly, and eventually became hopeless about the sad state of life. The state of things got so bad that the gods abandoned humans, letting them fend for themselves.

Pandora

FIRST MORTAL WOMAN ON EARTH

CLAIM TO FAME
She unleashed both good and bad things on humanity.

WHY SHE'S WEIRD
She was crafted out of clay.

A NEW WOMAN

Zeus punished Prometheus big-time for giving fire to humans. But he didn't stop there. He wanted to punish the people, too, for accepting the fire in the first place. So he concocted a plan to create the ideal woman, named Pandora, whose name means "all gifts." Zeus wanted to send her down to Earth to enchant humans and then unleash an evil into the world unlike any they'd ever seen. The master blacksmith Hephaestus

PANDORA IS SAID TO HAVE HAD

EYES MADE FROM SAPPHIRES AND LIPS MADE OF RED RUBIES.

Pandora may be a mythical character, but the lesson of her story is very real. Today, the phrase "to open a Pandora's box" is used frequently to describe how a person's actions may create an uncontrollable, bad situation. The term also highlights how even the most innocent curiosity can lead to danger if you're not careful. So next time you feel the urge to sneak into your big brother's off-limits room to play with his prized Lego collection? Take it from Pandora and keep out!

got to work molding her out of clay, and then the other gods stepped in to make her complete: Aphrodite gifted her with beauty, Apollo taught her how to sing and play instruments, Hermes taught her how to talk, and Athena fashioned her with intricately woven clothes.

UNBOXED

Hermes ushered Pandora down to Earth, where she enchanted both men and Titans alike. She was introduced to the foolish Titan Epimetheus, Prometheus's brother. Prometheus knew better than to accept any offer from Zeus, but his brother did not. He soon fell in love with Pandora and married her. As a wedding gift, Zeus presented the couple with a golden box. Inside, he'd planted all sorts of terrible things, like disease, hunger, war, greed, and sickness, to name a few. Zeus—knowing how curious Pandora was—told her to never, ever open the box. But Pandora just couldn't resist.

One day, she lifted up the lid of the box. Out came all of the bad stuff, the types of things that until that point had not existed on Earth. Knowing she'd made a huge mistake, Pandora slammed the lid of the box, but it was too late. Every terrible thing had escaped into the world. The one thing that stayed in the box? Hope. Some people believe that hope inside of the box symbolized keeping a glimmer of optimism when everything else seems so bleak and sad.

IT'S MYTHIC!
Some stories say Pandora's box was actually a clay jar known as a pithos.

73

The Fates

GODDESSES OF DESTINY

CLAIM TO FAME
The Fates controlled the lives of mortals, from birth to death.

WHY THEY'RE WEIRD These spinsters used magical thread to spin human destiny.

HAVE FATE

Talk about having all the power! These gray-haired women were responsible for determining how long each mortal would live. It was an ability that not even the gods could top—once the Fates determined your future, there was nothing anyone could do about it. And if you tried to meddle with their work? You'd have to answer to the Furies (see the next page)!

WEB OF LIFE

The Fates had a funny way of figuring out the course of one's life. They'd weave it! When someone was born, they would spin the thread of life and continue to weave that person's destinies until determining when to end it all.

SISTER ACT

The trio worked in concert to weave their powerful web.

CLOTHO: She spun the thread of life.

LACHESIS: She measured the length.

ATROPOS: She cut the thread to symbolize death.

IT'S MYTHIC!

The Fates would visit a baby three days after his or her birth to determine the course of his or her life.

SOME SAY THAT THE FATES' POWER WAS EVEN GREATER THAN ZEUS'S.

The Furies

GODDESSES OF REVENGE

CLAIM TO FAME
They punished wrongdoers by driving them mad.

WHY THEY'RE WEIRD The Furies had snakes for hair and carried whips made out of scorpions.

THE FURIES WERE BORN FROM THE BLOOD OF URANUS AFTER HE WAS WOUNDED BY HIS SON CRONUS.

HARD WORK

SPOOKY SISTERS

Just the frightful sight of this snake-haired trio could make you shudder, but their actions were even more terrifying. These ladies lived to represent justice by punishing any mortals who'd committed a serious crime like murder or harming a family member. The Furies spent their time lurking in the Underworld, taking orders from Hades, and inflicting so much torture on their victims that the victims would often wind up going crazy as a result.

CHANGE OF HEART

According to one story, Athena had a role in softening the sisters. After the trio sought to plague Orestes for murdering his mother in revenge for killing his father, Athena stepped in. She decided to give the mortal another chance, and then she soothed the revenge-seeking Furies. She even gave them a home in Athens where they worked to protect the city from danger and became known as Eumenides, or the "calm ones."

chill out

Like the Fates, each sister had a specific job in the Underworld. Here's more about their devilish duties:

MEGAERA:
"The Jealous One."
She went after the liars and the cheaters.

TISIPHONE:
"The Blood Avenger."
She punished crimes of murder, waiting to pluck her victims at the gates of Tartarus in a dress soaked with blood.

ALEKTO:
"The Furious One."
She sought revenge on anyone who committed a crime out of anger, especially against a family member.

IT'S MYTHIC!
The Furies are also referred to as the Three Erinyes.

Minor Gods

THE SUPPORTING PLAYERS

Aside from the main players on Mount Olympus, Greek mythology tells of many other gods who also had special powers, although far less powerful than the major gods (think of them as having a supporting role among the shining stars of the Olympians and Titans). Also known as minor gods, they laid claim to very small territories—like a stream or a single tree—as opposed to heftier jobs, like, say, controlling all of the weather in the universe. So who were some of these minor gods? Here's a cheat sheet of some to remember their roles and responsibilities.

CURETES

Goddesses of the wild mountainside, the Curetes were warriors that sprung from the ground fully dressed in armor and carrying weapons.

THE NYMPHS

Beautiful, enchanting women who usually lived in outdoor settings: among the trees, or in clouds, in rivers, or on beaches

ARISTAEUS

The god of fruit trees and bee-keeping, Aristaeus also mastered the art of curdling milk.

It's said that Aristaeus made the first goat milk cheese.

78

Asclepius once healed a snake, who in turn shared all of its secret wisdom (at the time, snakes were revered for their healing powers).

ASCLEPIUS

One of the master centaur Chiron's pupils, Asclepius was the god of medicine. He had such a powerful touch that he could heal people, then bring them back from the Underworld.

HARMONIA

Yep, you guessed it! Harmonia was the goddess of harmony, and the daughter of Aphrodite and Ares.

hello, gorgeous

NEMESIS

Goddess of retribution, or punishing arrogant people

Annoyed by Narcissus—a boy obsessed with his own image—Nemesis led him to a pool where Narcissus fell in love with his reflection ... and wound up dying of a broken heart because his reflection could never love him back.

7 Gods of Personification

The ancient Greeks attributed everything they said and did to the gods. Got a great night of sleep before a big test? There's a god behind that. Found a $10 bill on the street? Ditto. Basically, each everyday emotion and action can be represented—or personified—by a particular god. Here are seven gods that the Greeks honored and looked to for guidance.

PLOUTOS

THE PERSONIFICATION OF:
Wealth

It's said Zeus took away Ploutos's sight so that he'd dole out dollars blindly and without favoritism.

CAERUS

THE PERSONIFICATION OF:
Opportunity

Catch him if you can! Caerus had super speed and could fly, thanks to winged feet.

Caerus is depicted in art as having a single lock of hair. This represented fleeting opportunity: If you didn't grasp that piece of hair, you'd quickly lose your chance at a good thing.

We get the word "hypnosis"—which is when someone is put in a sleeplike state—from this god.

HYPNOS

THE PERSONIFICATION OF: Sleep

The son of Nyx (the deity of night) and Erebus (darkness), Hypnos visited people in the wee hours to ease them into a state of rest.

ΝΙΚΣ

THE PERSONIFICATION OF: Victory

Nike earned her rep by helping the Olympians snag victory in the battle against the Titans.

The famed sneaker company borrowed its name from this winged goddess.

ΔΙΚΣ

THE PERSONIFICATION OF: Justice

Dike, shown as a blindfolded young woman holding a balance scale, ruled over human justice.

Born a mortal, Dike was eventually brought up to Mount Olympus by Zeus after realizing that keeping mankind just was an impossible task.

ΣΙΡΣΝΣ

THE PERSONIFICATION OF: Peace

The daughter of Zeus and the Titan Themis, Eirene is often depicted holding an olive branch, a symbol of peace.

ΜΣΤΙS

THE PERSONIFICATION OF: Cleverness

Metis, the first wife of Zeus, was said to be the wisest of all mortals and gods.

Chiron

THE KING OF THE CENTAURS

CLAIM TO FAME

He was the legendary teacher of many Greek heroes.

WHY HE'S WEIRD

He was half man and half horse.

FATHER FIGURE

Behind every great hero and god is a great ... centaur? At least this was the case with Chiron, who groomed many of the most accomplished mortals—and immortals—in mythology. Here's a rundown of his star pupils:

ASCLEPIUS: Chiron taught this god of healing the art of surgery as well as how to use medicine.

ACHILLES: Chiron fed him the meat of lions and bears to make him brave and taught him how to ride horses and hunt.

JASON: Chiron took an infant Jason under his wing—er, hoof—and tutored him in astrology, which later helped him in his quest to recover the Golden Fleece. (See page 101 for the full story.)

HERACLES: Chiron equipped the powerful demigod with the skills he needed to complete his 12 heroic tasks. (See page 86 for more info on that.)

TEACHER TO HEROES

Chiron wasn't your average centaur: The son of the Titan Cronus and a sea nymph, he was super smart, kind, and not violent like the other centaurs galloping around. Over time, he became known for his wisdom, and famous Greek heroes like Heracles, Jason, and Achilles came to seek his knowledge. He taught them math and science, including the art of healing. The ancient Greeks believed that without Chiron, there would be no medicine.

IT'S MYTHIC!

Where did Chiron get his wit? Myth says Apollo adopted the centaur as an infant and taught him everything he knew.

LIFE SWAP

As a son of Cronus, Chiron was immortal. Yet he still felt pain. And when one of Heracles' poisonous arrows accidentally pierced his knee, it hurt so much, Chiron begged to die. The only problem? He couldn't (that's the tricky part about living forever!). But Chiron still found a way to rid himself of his pain. Here's the story.

Remember how Zeus punished Prometheus for giving fire to man? He bound him to a rock and ordered a giant bird to peck at the Titan's liver all day every day. The only way Zeus would agree to release Prometheus from his torment was if an immortal offered to go to Tartarus in Prometheus's place. Seeing no other way to rid himself of his incurable wound, Chiron gave up his immortality for Prometheus and headed to Tartarus, where he died and was finally free from pain. Eventually, Zeus launched him to the heavens, giving him eternal afterlife among the stars.

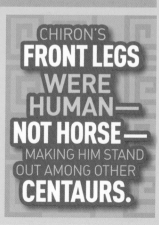

CHIRON'S **FRONT LEGS** WERE **HUMAN— NOT HORSE—** MAKING HIM STAND OUT AMONG OTHER **CENTAURS.**

Heracles

A MORTAL HERO TURNED GOD

CLAIM TO FAME

He was the most famous hero in mythology—and the only one to earn immortality.

WHY HE'S WEIRD He fought centaurs, slayed a sea monster, and tamed man-eating mares all for the chance to live forever.

SO STRONG

The son of Zeus and the mortal Alcmena, Heracles (also spelled Hercules) had it rough from the start. Enraged that Zeus had a child with another woman, Hera wished nothing but evil on the infant. So when he was just eight months old, she unleashed a pair of giant snakes into his room. Imagine her surprise when Heracles grabbed each snake by the throat and strangled them with his tiny hands. Indeed, this child with superhuman strength was special. Hera had her work cut out for her.

BAD BEHAVIOR

Heracles had a temper as powerful as his muscles, and sometimes couldn't control his own strength. Case in point? The time his music tutor corrected him as he played the lute. In a fit of frustration, Heracles smashed the instrument over the tutor's head with a blow so hard it killed him. He felt horrible, but the deadly deed was done. As a punishment, Heracles was sent to live on a cattle ranch until he turned 18.

MAD DAD

Eventually, Heracles married Megara, the daughter of a mortal king, and the couple had three sons. Once Hera caught wind of this exciting news, she made it her mission to squash Heracles' happiness. So she cursed the demigod with a sudden madness that he couldn't control and caused him to kill his beloved family. Once Heracles snapped out of the trance and realized what he had done, he fell into a deep despair. He begged to be forgiven for his evil ways. An oracle—or future-teller—told Heracles that he would have to serve King Eurystheus and complete 12 tasks in 12 years. Once Heracles completed this to-do list, he would be forgiven and become immortal.

MODERN MYTHOLOGY
WHAT'S A HERO?

Strength, power, courage, and heart: Many of the qualities that heroes in Greek mythology boast are similar to those of the most famous gods. Like gods, Greek heroes were far from perfect: They'd often lie, cheat, and steal to get the job done. But they differ in that heroes are often mortal, being only half-related to a god. And they're typically defined by one major challenge or task (like Heracles' 12 labors) rather than a lifetime of fantastic feats.

THE CONSTELLATION HERCULES IS THE FIFTH LARGEST ONE IN THE SKY.

LIST OF LABORS

Heracles had to go to heroic lengths to win forgiveness—
and immortality—from the gods after his bad behavior. Here's a list of
his (almost) impossible to-dos—and how he got them done.

TASK # ① SLAY THE NEMEAN LION, WHICH HAD BEEN STALKING THE COUNTRYSIDE.

THE DETAILS: After an unsuccessful attempt at shooting the lion with his arrows, Heracles chased it into a cave and killed the beast with his hands. He then used the lion's hide as a protective cloak.

TASK # ②

KILL THE LERNAEAN HYDRA, A NINE-HEADED SWAMP MONSTER WITH POISONOUS BLOOD.

THE DETAILS: Heracles wrestled the Hydra to the ground, striking each head with his club. The trouble was, each time he sliced off a head, another two grew. So Heracles recruited his nephew Iolaus to help him out. Using a burning torch, the pair seared each of Hydra's necks after lopping off a head, finally killing the monster.

TASK # ③

CAPTURE A CERYNEIAN HIND, A SWIFT DEER WITH GOLDEN HORNS.

THE DETAILS: The deer was so fast, it took Heracles an entire year before he was able to nab it in a net as it crossed a stream.

TASK # ④

KILL THE GIANT ERYMANTHIAN BOAR.

THE DETAILS: Heracles snagged the boar by trapping it in deep snow and tying it up in chains.

TASK # ⑤

CLEAN OUT THE AUGEAN STABLES, FILLED WITH 30 YEARS' WORTH OF HORSE MANURE—IN ONE DAY.

THE DETAILS: It was a dirty (and stinky!) job, but nothing Heracles couldn't handle. His trick? Cutting holes in the sides of the stables so that a nearby river flowed right through them, flushing out all of the poop overnight.

TASK # ⑥

SCARE AWAY THE DEADLY STYMPHALIAN BIRDS.

THE DETAILS: These birds were beasts! Their droppings killed crops, their metal-tipped feathers could slice an unsuspecting passerby, and they actually ate people and animals. Heracles finished off the flock by first shaking them from the trees, then shooting them with poison arrows as they tried to fly away.

TASK # ⑦

FETCH THE FAMOUS WILD BULL OF CRETE.

THE DETAILS: This was somewhat of a simple task for Heracles. He captured the beautiful white bull alive and showed it to the king before releasing it. Done and done.

TASK # ⑧

BRING BACK THE MAN-EATING MARES OF DIOMEDES.

THE DETAILS: Heracles had to work extra hard to trap these heinous horses, which belonged to Diomedes, the king of Thrace. Once he fought Diomedes' army and killed the king, Heracles calmed the mares down enough to herd them back to King Eurystheus.

TASK # ⑨

STEAL THE BELT OF HIPPOLYTA, THE QUEEN OF THE AMAZONS.

THE DETAILS: To snag the belt of this mighty queen, Heracles set sail to the land of the Amazons and charmed her into giving him her belt. Angered over this easy exchange, Hera transformed herself into an Amazon and encouraged this tribe of female warriors to attack Heracles. Having no other choice, Heracles would end up killing Hippolyta.

TASK # ⑩

FETCH THE CATTLE OF GERYON, A THREE-HEADED MONSTER.

THE DETAILS: Heracles traveled to the remote island ruled by Geryon, a three-headed, six-legged herdsmen. Once there, he clubbed the monster (and his two-headed guard dog), then brought the cattle home.

TASK # (11) FETCH GOLDEN APPLES FROM THE TREE GUARDED BY THE HESPERIDES NYMPHS.

THE DETAILS: These apples—Hera's wedding gift to Zeus—grew on a tree in the garden of the gods, where they were guarded by a dragon and a trio of nymphs. Heracles sought advice from Prometheus, who suggested he ask Atlas for help, since the nymphs were Atlas's daughters. The two worked out a plan: Heracles would hold up the sky for Atlas, who would then slip into the garden and dupe his daughters into giving him the apples. Atlas was so desperate for a rest from his backbreaking task that he agreed. The ploy worked, and Heracles was then able to present the magical fruit to King Eurystheus.

MODERN MYTHOLOGY
HAND IT OVER

No doubt, Heracles was a giant among his peers. And historians believe that the ancient world honored this mega-man with a supersize statue that possibly stood taller than a four-story building! Constructed between A.D. 162 and 166, this marble sculpture stood outside a temple to Heracles (aka Hercules) in what is now modern-day Jordan. A catastrophic earthquake likely destroyed the statue, but two pivotal pieces remain: three giant fingers and an elbow. Also known as the "Hand of Hercules," this fragment is now one of antiquity's most revered sculptures. While experts can only guess what the rest of the sculpture looked like, all fingers point to the fact that it was easily one of the largest marble statues to have ever existed.

TASK # (12)

FETCH THE DOG CERBERUS FROM HADES.

THE DETAILS: Heracles descended into Hades and wounded the god of the Underworld so severely that he had to go up to Olympus in search of a cure. In his weakened state, Hades told Heracles that he could borrow his dog as long as he could catch him without using a weapon. Up for the challenge, Heracles managed to wrangle the dog and drag him out of the Underworld. When he showed Cerberus to the king, Eurystheus was so scared at the sight of the ferocious dog that he leapt into an urn.

Perseus

THE SLAYER OF MONSTERS

CLAIM TO FAME
He killed the snake-haired Medusa, who could turn men into stone.

WHY HE'S WEIRD Perseus could fly, thanks to the winged sandals he borrowed from Hermes.

not cool, Dad

PERSEUS MARRIED HIS WIFE, **ANDROMEDA**, AFTER **RESCUING HER** FROM A **SEA MONSTER.**

MODERN MYTHOLOGY
BOOK IT

What do you get when the myth of Perseus meets fiction? Percy Jackson! The superpopular book series is based on the stories of Perseus "Percy" Jackson, son of Poseidon. Like the mythical Perseus, Percy faces off with the Titan Atlas. He also has a run-in with Medusa, although in the modern version, she's a shop-owner named Aunt Em, not a horrible-looking monster. But, like his mythical namesake, Percy chops off her head just before she can turn him to stone.

HEAD GAMES

The rumors of his fate started before Perseus was born. An oracle said that Perseus—son of a mortal, Danae, and Zeus—would grow up and kill his grandfather King Acrisius. Fearing that this prophecy would come true, the king sent Perseus and his mother out to sea. They eventually washed up on the island of Seriphos, where a local king named Polydectes eventually fell in love with Danae. Ever protective of his mother, Perseus promised the king that he'd present him with the head of Medusa if he would leave his mom alone. Polydectes agreed. But how would Perseus ever capture the snake-headed monster who could turn humans to stone?

Myth says that the real-life Atlas Mountains were formed when Perseus waved Medusa's head in front of the Titan Atlas, turning him to stone.

ON A MISSION

Slaying Medusa became Perseus's (almost) impossible mission. As Zeus's son, he had access to the gods who offered to help him out. Athena told him that he would have to go to the Graeae, three goddesses who shared one eye and one tooth among them—and who just so happened to be Medusa's sisters. Perseus sneakily stole their eye and tooth and told them that they'd never see or eat again if they didn't offer up Medusa's location. Begrudgingly, the terrifying trio led Perseus to Medusa's cave hideout.

STONE FACED

But first, Perseus had to prep for battle against this petrifying monster. Again, the gods stepped in, providing him with a collection of tools including winged sandals, which allowed him to fly; an unbreakable sickle; a reflective bronze shield; a helmet of invisibility; and a bag big enough to hold Medusa's head. Armed with these items, Perseus snuck up on Medusa while she slept, holding up the shield by his shoulder so that he could see her in the reflection without having to make direct eye contact. With one swipe of his sickle, he cut off her head and tossed it into his giant bag.

But that's not where this story ends. As soon as Perseus cut off Medusa's head, out popped two of her sons with Poseidon: a warrior named Chrysaor and the winged horse Pegasus. To make a quick escape, Perseus jumped on Pegasus and flew back to Seriphos. Once there, he waved the head of Medusa in front of King Polydectes and turned him to stone.

YOU CAN'T ΣSCAPΣ FATE

Hailed as a hero for slaying Medusa, then winning the heart of the beautiful Andromeda, it seemed like Perseus had found his happily ever after. But that pesky prophecy about him killing his grandfather Acrisius just wouldn't go away. In fact, years later, while participating in a discus-throwing contest, Perseus accidentally hit his grandfather, fatally injuring him and fulfilling the prophecy.

Bellerophon

CLAIM TO FAME
He slayed the fire-breathing Chimera.

WHY HE'S WEIRD His best friend was Pegasus, a flying horse.

ONE MYTH TELLS OF BELLEROPHON **TAKING DOWN** A **FIERCE PIRATE** WHO'D BEEN **STALKING** THE SEAS.

BEASTLY BATTLE

Who's afraid of a fire-breathing monster? Not Bellerophon, who sealed his status as a mythological hero by slaying the Chimera, a beast that fed on the people in the town of Lycia. Tasked to do the job by King Iobates, the brave Bellerophon battled the beast and essentially saved thousands of people from getting gobbled up.

But the challenge was not conquered easily. Like his fellow demigods, Bellerophon got some help before completing his heroic tasks. After a fortune-teller told Bellerophon to use the magical winged horse Pegasus to slay the Chimera, Bellerophon approached Athena for assistance. She gave him a golden bridle, which he could use to capture and ride Pegasus.

BREATH OF HOT AIR

Together, they flew to the Chimera's lair, Bellerophon armed with a spear tipped with a block of lead he'd gathered from Earth. When he plunged the spear into the Chimera's throat, the beast's burning breath melted the lead and the molten substance suffocated him.

A STINGING BLOW

As Bellerophon's fame grew, so did his head. He got so bold that he decided it'd be no big deal if he rode Pegasus up to Mount Olympus. His hope? That the gods would honor him and his heroic ways. But Zeus wasn't really impressed. So he sent a fly to sting Pegasus, who bucked with the pain and tossed Bellerophon off his back. The hero plummeted down to Earth, where he landed in a heap, injured but still alive. From that point on, he hobbled around the Earth searching for his beloved horse.

MODERN MYTHOLOGY PLANETARY MOTION

Look up at the night sky and you just may see a strange, sparkling object that looks a lot like a wobbling star. Nicknamed Bellerophon, this quick-moving gas giant (it's 150 times more massive than Earth!) is the first planet outside our solar system to orbit a sun-like star. Life on Bellerophon is anything but sunny, though. Liquid iron falls like rain, and temperatures top 3000°F (1649°C). Sounds like a perfect fit for a powerful hero!

IT'S MYTHIC!

Myths say that Pegasus wound up with the gods, carrying Zeus's thunder and lightning across the sky.

Theseus

THE HERO OF ATHENS

CLAIM TO FAME
He saved his kingdom—and the lives of children—by destroying the Minotaur.

WHY HE'S WEIRD Theseus is said to have started the sport of wrestling by challenging his enemies to a tussle.

HEIR APPARENT

King Aegeus of Athens was handsome, rich, and lived in the lap of luxury. When he married Aethra, the daughter of another king, it seemed like he had all he could ever want, except one thing: an heir—a son, to be exact. But not just any son. The prince that would take over his throne had to be amazing, talented, impressively strong, and wise. So when King Aegeus eventually had his son Theseus, he wouldn't let the prince claim his birthright until he proved himself powerful and savvy enough to be the heir to the Athenian throne.

IT'S MYTHIC!

Theseia, a popular ancient Greek festival, celebrated Theseus with parades and athletic games.

BECOMING A HERO

To elevate himself to hero status, Theseus got to work immediately. Displaying dazzling smarts and strength, he began to take down the town's criminals. He sought out scoundrels and thieves, doling out the same sort of punishment they inflicted on innocent victims. He wrestled some, tossed others over cliffs, and made the town's roads safe from robbers. Pretty soon, Theseus became known throughout the land as a hero and King Aegeus accepted him as his son and heir.

POWER PLAY

Theseus couldn't have come into power at a better time. Defeated by Crete in battle, Athens was obligated by the king of Crete to sacrifice seven girls and seven boys every nine years. These kids—also known as tributes—were offered up as food for the Minotaur, a heinous half man, half bull who lived in a maze known as the Labyrinth. If Athens didn't oblige? The city would be destroyed.

The premise of The Hunger Games, a top-selling book and movie series, is heavily influenced by the Greek myth of Theseus and the Minotaur. In fact, the books' author, Suzanne Collins, said that she was struck by the story when she first heard it as a child and later reimagined it to use as inspiration for her famous books. In Collins's version, 24 children—one boy and one girl from 12 districts—are chosen as tributes to battle in the Hunger Games in order to appease a powerful central government.

UNWOUND AND UNBOUND

To save the children of Athens from this horrible fate, Theseus hatched his next heroic move. He offered to go to Crete in place of one of the kids. Once there, he'd slay the Minotaur. It wouldn't be easy, of course. First, he had to navigate the Labyrinth. Armed with a ball of golden thread given to him by the king of Crete's daughter Ariadne, he tied one end to the entrance door of the Labyrinth, then slowly unspooled the thread as he walked. That way, he could retrace his steps when he turned to leave.

Once in the Labyrinth, Theseus found the Minotaur asleep. He crept up to the monster and began beating it with his bare fists, packing powerful wallops with each punch. Then he used his sword to finish off the beast. Theseus then navigated the children out of the maze and on to safety following the long piece of golden string he left behind.

SAIL AWAY

Before Theseus left for Crete, King Aegeus told him that upon returning to Athens, he was to fly a white sail if he slayed the Minotaur. And if he didn't? The ship's crew should raise a black sail. Forgetting his father's request, Theseus flew a black sail as he cruised into Athens. Spotting the sails and assuming the worst, a grief-stricken Aegeus threw himself off a cliff into the sea, making Theseus the new king of Athens—and giving the Aegean Sea its name.

TRAGIC ENDING

As king of Athens, Theseus took the first step toward creating the first democracy of the known world by transferring many of his powers as king over to an elected assembly. He also helped the poor. Yet for all the good he did, Theseus was not given a true happy ending. While visiting the island of Scyros, the king Lycomedes—a so-called friend of Theseus—pushed him off a cliff, fearful that the heroic king would overtake his throne.

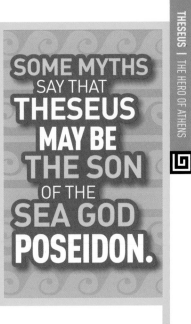

SOME MYTHS SAY THAT **THESEUS MAY BE THE SON** OF THE **SEA GOD POSEIDON.**

nooooooo!

Jason

THE WANDERER OF THE SEA

CLAIM TO FAME He defeated a dragon to grab the Golden Fleece of a magical winged lamb.

WHY HE'S WEIRD He was raised by Chiron, a centaur, on a mountaintop.

A PRINCE IS BORN

Imagine being born into royalty, but to never be able to claim that birthright because your evil uncle wants nothing to do with you. That's what happened to Jason. Born a prince of Iolcus, Jason was soon spirited away to live with the wise centaur Chiron to keep him hidden from the murderous wrath of his uncle Pelias (who had already killed Jason's father to overtake the throne). Life wasn't all that bad, though: Chiron took great care of Jason, giving him all the tools he needed to become a courageous and accomplished adult.

A ROYAL RETURN

By the time he turned 20, Jason was ready to embrace his royal status. So he headed to Iolcus to face off with Pelias and demand his throne. Pelias offered Jason a challenge: If he brought back the Golden Fleece of a sacred winged lamb that lived in Colchis, located at the edge of the world, he'd turn over the kingdom. Jason accepted the challenge as Pelias laughed behind his back, believing that the mission was truly impossible. After all, the fleece was guarded by a dragon that never slept!

Of course, Pelias didn't give his nephew enough credit. Jason acted immediately, gathering together all of the great heroes to crew a 50-oared ship called the *Argo*. Together the Argonauts navigated rough waters and brutal battles on their way to find the fleece.

MODERN MYTHOLOGY
THE GOLDEN TRUTH

The Golden Fleece may not be just a thing of fantasy! According to geologists who did fieldwork in a region off the east coast of the Black Sea, the kingdom of Colchis was in fact ripe with gold. And, they say, people living in this area often used sheepskin to capture small pieces of gold in rivers. The result? A fleece studded with gold! The researchers also believe that Jason's famous tale may have been inspired by an actual gold-seeking voyage that took place some 3,500 years ago.

JASON SHOWED OFF HIS **HEROIC SIDE** AS A KID WHEN HE **CARRIED AN ELDERLY WOMAN** ACROSS A **SWIFT-MOVING STREAM.**

SAIL ON

It wasn't a simple journey from Iolcus to Colchis. Here's some of the wacky stuff Jason and the Argonauts ran into along the way:

LENGTHY PIT STOP:

Their first stop was Lemnos, an island filled with women who had been cast off there after Aphrodite cursed them with an awful smell for refusing to worship her. The Lemnos ladies saw the Argonauts as fathers for future children, and after a few years, the island had been repopulated.

CONFUSING WINDS:

After sailing off from their second stop in the land of the Doliones, a storm swooped in and turned the boat completely around. When the *Argo* ran aground back at the land of the Doliones in the middle of the night, the island's inhabitants mistook the crew for enemies and attacked. The Argonauts wound up accidentally slaying the island's king.

LOST CREW:

After one of the ship's men, Hylas, went to fetch freshwater from their third port of Mysia, he was kidnapped by a nymph. Heracles dashed into the island's thick forests to find his friend, but he couldn't do so in time. The *Argo* sailed off without them.

BOX, THEN BATTLE:

In the land of Bebrykes, the king challenged one of the Argonauts, Polydeuces, to a boxing match. Polydeuces wound up killing the king in the ring, causing a battle between the Bebrykes and the Argonauts, who fled as quickly as they could.

STINKY BIRDS:

On their fifth stop in Salmydessus, the Argonauts encountered a blind prophet named Phineus. He was having a heck of a time with Harpies, birds with the faces of women. These annoying animals tormented Phineus by pooping on his food every time he tried to eat and leaving behind a super-stinky scent. Seeing the starving and struggling soothsayer, Jason offered to get rid of the Harpies if Phineus would give him a glimpse into the future. So the Argonauts drove the Harpies to another island while Jason and crew caught a sneak peek into the near future, which helped them conquer their next challenge. And Phineus was never tormented again.

ROCK AND ROLL:

To get to Colchis, the *Argo* had to pass through a narrow area of enormous moving rocks and crashing waves known as the Symplegades. To get past this treacherous place, Jason released a dove first to find a safe path. Following the direction of the dove, the Argonauts rowed as hard and fast as they could to follow, barely making it through to the other side.

ALL FOR THE FLEECE

But all of that was just the beginning. When they finally arrived in Colchis, the king who had been keeping the Golden Fleece presented Jason with yet *another* set of challenges. These included plowing a field with two fire-breathing bulls, sowing the field with dragon teeth, fighting off warriors who protected those fields, and defeating the dragon that guarded the fleece. The king was confident that there was no way Jason would ever complete these tasks, but again, the joke was on him: Turns out the king's daughter, a sorceress named Medea, fell in love with Jason and offered to help him if he married her.

HELLAS

1995

ΕΛΛΗΝΙΚΗ ΔΗΜΟΚΡΑΤΙΑ 200

FALL FROM THE THRONE

Finally, Jason earned the right to his father's throne—and he brought Medea along to serve beside him. While the people certainly appreciated Jason, Medea was another story. They didn't like her sorcery and wanted her gone—eventually forcing the pair to hide out in the city of Corinth. That's when things got really rocky: Jason eventually betrayed Medea by marrying another woman. Furious, Medea cursed Jason's new wife and children, killing them. While mourning the loss of his family, Jason retreated to his famed boat, the *Argo*. While there, he was struck in the head by a rotted-out piece of the boat, and died suddenly.

NO TASK TOO TOUGH

An impossible job? Not if you're Jason! Here's how this hero—and his sorceress sidekick—did the unthinkable.

THE TASK: Plow a field with two fire-breathing bulls and scatter dragon teeth.

THE SOLUTION: Medea mixed up a magical ointment that gave Jason superpowered strength and protected him from the oxen's flames.

THE TASK: Fight off weapon-wielding warriors trying to protect their field.

THE SOLUTION: Using his brute strength, Jason heaved a stone into the field, sending the soldiers scattering. Then, not knowing where the rock originated from, the soldiers turned on each other, distracting them from Jason.

THE TASK: Fight off a dragon guarding the Golden Fleece.

THE SOLUTION: Medea used her sorcery to hypnotize the three-tongued dragon. When it fell asleep, Jason quietly picked up the Golden Fleece and snuck it back onto the *Argo*.

Odysseus

THE TRAVELING KING

CLAIM TO FAME
Inventor of the Trojan Horse

WHY HE'S WEIRD

He spent 10 years traveling home after winning the Trojan War.

AT WAR

Odysseus, the ruler of the island kingdom of Ithaca, was known as a clever and cunning king. During his reign, the people of Troy—known as Trojans—and the Greeks were battling a war sparked by the capture of the Spartan queen Helen (see page 56). To win the war and bring Helen home, the Greeks first had to make their way past the wall surrounding Troy. The wall was so tall and strong, breaking through it seemed impossible.

WHEN HE **RETURNED** FROM WAR AND HIS LONG JOURNEY HOME, ODYSSEUS'S **DOG RECOGNIZED** **HIM**—20 YEARS LATER!

welcome home!

FAR AFIELD

Meanwhile, Odysseus was doing all he could to avoid going to war. In fact, to avoid war, he pretended he had gone insane! He hitched his donkey to a plow and began sowing his fields with salt instead of seeds. People were onto him, though. To test his mental well-being, a man placed his infant son in front of Odysseus's plow. When the king made an abrupt turn to avoid the baby, it proved his mental state was quite sound—and poor Odysseus reluctantly headed to battle.

HORSING AROUND

The Trojan War raged on for 10 long years. Just when it all seemed hopeless, Odysseus had his best idea yet: In order to break into Troy, they would build a huge wooden horse, leave it by the gate of the walled city, and pretend to retreat. If Odysseus's plan worked, the Trojans would think the horse was their "prize" and bring it inside their gate. Little did they know, inside the hollow horse, dozens of Greek troops would be lying in wait. Once the Trojans brought the horse past the gate, they'd leap out, ready to pounce.

It was the perfect plan. The people of Troy gladly accepted the stunning horse, displaying it at the center of their city. At night, as everyone in town was sound asleep, the men hiding inside climbed out, opened the gates, and let the Greek army into Troy to nab Helen. Thanks to Odysseus, the Greeks won the Trojan War, and it was time for the hero to head home.

MODERN MYTHOLOGY
POPULAR POEM

The adventures of Odysseus became famous through the epic poem written by the blind Greek poet Homer in the eighth century B.C. Today, *The Odyssey* has been translated into 250 different languages and 45 million copies of the book have been sold worldwide.

I come in peace ...

AN EPIC JOURNEY

After 10 long years, Odysseus and his men started
the return journey to their home of Ithaca, which should've been
a quick trip. But a huge storm pushed Odysseus and his men
off course. After that, here's what they had in store:

A CAVE-DWELLING CYCLOPS

For a bunch of hungry soldiers, finding
a cave full of sheep was a major
score. Odysseus and his crew
thought they had it made when
they captured a few of the animals for dinner, roasting them on
a stick over a fire. Just as they
settled in to eat, a one-eyed
giant, also known as a Cyclops,
came roaring out of the cave
swinging a club, angry that the
soldiers stole his sheep. A
quick-thinking Odysseus used his
stick to blind the Cyclops. Then he and
his men escaped from the cave—and the
blind Cyclops—by each clinging to the belly
of a sheep, and literally holding on for their lives.

EVIL MERMAIDS

What's that sound? While sailing
along, Odysseus heard the dreaded
song of the Sirens, creatures with
the bodies of birds, the faces
and voices of women,
and many evil inten-
tions. Typically, the
Sirens would hypnotize
sailors into a stunned
state with their song. And,
without anyone steering the
ship, the sailors would crash
and die. But not Odysseus. This
smarty knew the scary truth
about the Sirens and stuffed his
ears—and the ears of his crew—
with beeswax. They sailed safely on.

DEADLY BEASTS

Talk about a double whammy! While attempting to pass through a narrow stretch of sea, Odysseus faced not one, but two monsters stalking both sides of the shore. On one side: Scylla, a ghastly ghoul with six heads on snaky necks, her mouth full of spiky teeth. On the other: Charybdis, a sea monster who whipped the ocean into a powerful whirlpool.

As he guided the ship through the channel, Odysseus barely missed getting snapped up by Scylla, only to get tossed into the swirling water after encountering Charybdis. He survived by clinging to a tree near the ocean, then managed to make it back to the ship once the whirlpool spat it back up.

A SNEAKY WITCH

When you've been traveling for years and a witch invites you over for dinner, it's hard to say no. Especially if you have no idea she's actually evil. That's what happened to Odysseus and his men when they took a break on the island of Aeaea, where they met with a stunning enchantress named Circe. She had the habit of turning humans into animals (her palace was guarded by lions, bears, and wolves—all former men she had transformed), and couldn't resist casting a spell on the sailors. Although Odysseus passed on the meal, some of his men gobbled up her food, which happened to be laced with a magical potion that turned them into pigs. To get his friends back into human form, Odysseus sought the help of the god Hermes, who gave him a special herb that protected him from Circe's spells. Odysseus confronted the witch, threatened her with his sword, and forced her to flip his friends back into people.

A VERY LONG SWIM

Odysseus wasn't just a good sailor—he could swim well, too. This skill came in handy when Zeus struck his ship with a thunderbolt, wrecking the ship and killing all of the crew except for Odysseus. Clutching onto the mast of the ship, Odysseus swam for 10 days before washing ashore on an island. Later, just before he returned home on a raft, Poseidon churned the seas with a strong storm, sending Odysseus swimming again. This time, he finally made it back to his home safely, reuniting with his wife, Penelope.

Legendary Lands

WHERE THE MYTHS TAKE PLACE

Ancient Greek mythology tells of many territories scattered throughout the country. These real-life places, also known as city-states, were mostly ruled by a king, and maintained their own customs and laws. The ancient Greeks believed that one or two gods kept a special eye on their land. They built temples in their towns to honor those gods. Here's more about some of the central city-states we hear about in so many myths.

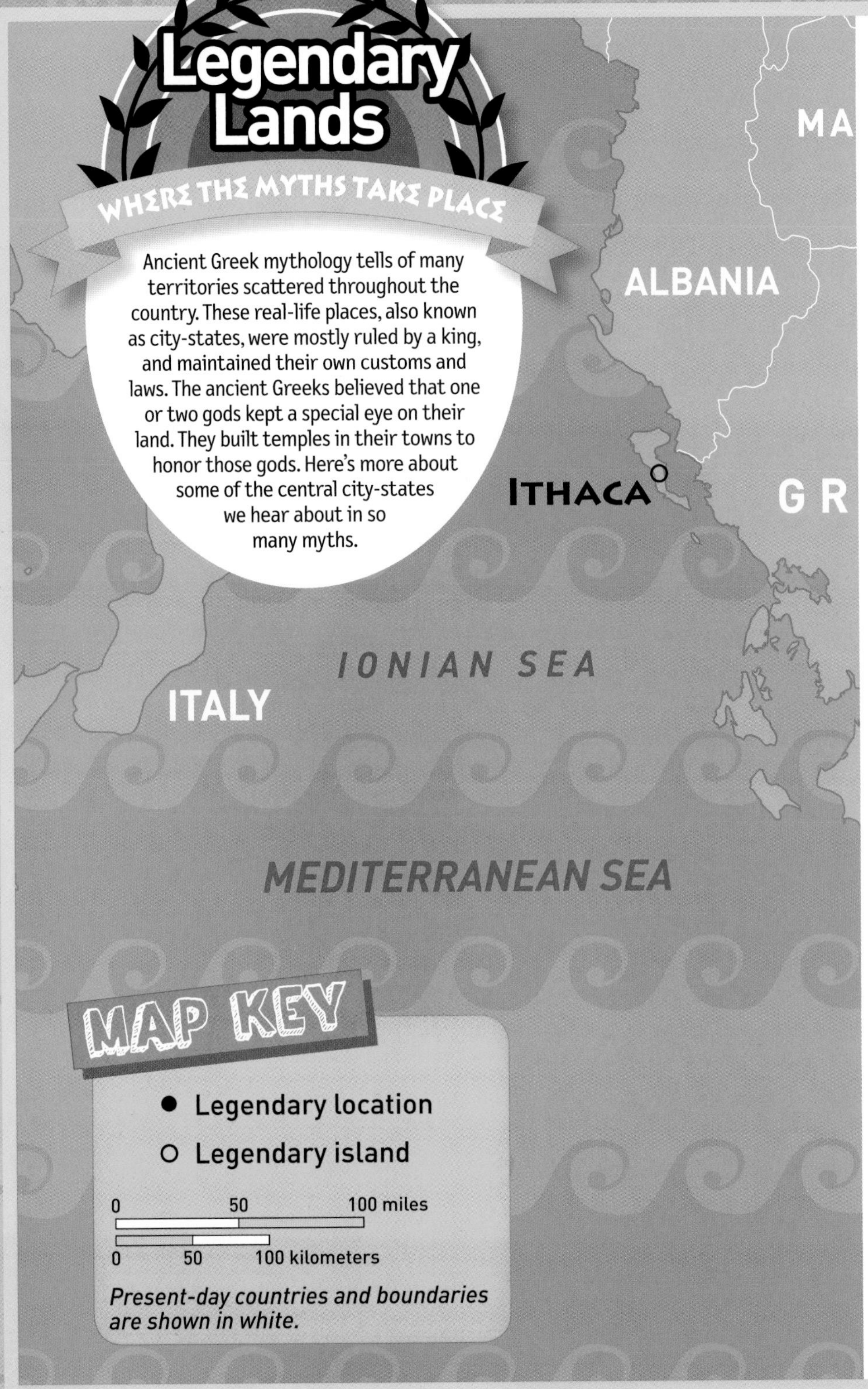

MA

ALBANIA

ITHACA

G R

IONIAN SEA

ITALY

MEDITERRANEAN SEA

MAP KEY

- ● Legendary location
- ○ Legendary island

```
0          50          100 miles
|----------|-----------|
0     50      100 kilometers
```

Present-day countries and boundaries are shown in white.

BULGARIA

CEDONIA

TURKEY

•MOUNT
OLYMPUS

TROY•

AEGEAN
SEA

EECE

DELPHI•

•THEBES

•ATHENS

•SPARTA

SEA OF CRETE

CRETE○

MEDITERRANEAN SEA

PICTURED HERE IS THE REAL-LIFE TROY, LOCATED ON THE NORTHWEST COAST OF MODERN-DAY TURKEY.

Troy

THE SITE OF THE TROJAN WAR

Situated on the coast of the Aegean Sea, Troy was once a bustling city operating within towering, nearly impenetrable walls, said to be built by the gods themselves. Homer's famous Greek poem *The Iliad* tells us most of what we know about mythological Troy, describing the final year of the decade-long Trojan War. After the Greeks and Trojans battled year after year, the gods ultimately decided the fate of this city, and Zeus demanded that it be destroyed. The end of the war marked the fall of Troy, when this once thriving city was ransacked and burned to the ground.

CLAIM TO FAME

After a 10-year battle over the kidnapping of Helen, the Spartan queen, Troy was eventually conquered by the Greek army during the Trojan War.

honk

ALONG CAME HELEN

In the city-state of Sparta lived a stunning princess named Helen. She was the daughter of Zeus and the mortal Lena, who was wooed by the king of gods as he was disguised as a swan. As a result, Helen was born out of an egg! Widely considered the most beautiful girl in the world, Helen grew up to marry Menelaus, the king of Sparta. Together, they had a daughter named Hermione and lived a peaceful existence—but their fairy-tale life did not last long.

Paris, the prince of Troy, had plans to kidnap Helen. Why? Because during a contest where he was asked to name the fairest god in all of Olympus, Aphrodite promised Paris the power to marry the most beautiful woman in the world if he picked her (see page 56). Helen, he believed, was rightfully his. So Paris headed to Sparta with many ships, where he was welcomed graciously by an unsuspecting King Menelaus. Meanwhile, Helen, under a love spell cast by Aphrodite, fled with Paris back to Troy late one night.

Realizing that his wife was gone, a heartbroken Menelaus declared war on Troy and vowed to win her back. The Greeks set sail toward Troy on 1,000 ships—which is why it's said that Helen had a "face that could launch a thousand ships."

THIS MEANS WAR!

The war was long and often seemed hopeless as neither side would budge. Both gods and mortals fought in the battle. The god Apollo refused to let the war end—he saw it as amusement and let it go on for way too long. Bloody battles would last all day long, only to end in a draw. Thousands and thousands of soldiers on both sides—including Paris—died on the battlefield.

HORSE PLAY

It wasn't until almost 10 years later that the Greek hero Odysseus came up with the idea to present the Trojans with a giant wooden horse—only to hide sneaky Greek soldiers inside to creep out and seize the city in the dark of night (for more of that story, flip to page 105). Once they had Helen, the Greeks burned the city to the ground.

WHEN GODS GET MAD

Troy seemed to be cursed long before it was destroyed by the Greeks. As punishment for offending Zeus, the gods Poseidon and Apollo were sent to the city to build its huge walls. Troy's king, Laomedon, promised to pay them in exchange for their labor, but he didn't keep that promise. This enraged the gods, leading Poseidon to send a sea monster to attack Troy and soak all of its fields with salt water. Later on, Poseidon carried his grudge against Laomedon into the Trojan War and sided with the Greek army. Sounds like Laomedon learned a valuable lesson: Never get on the bad side of a Greek god!

FACT OR FICTION?

Did the Trojan War actually occur—or is it just a myth? Experts aren't so sure. The poet Homer discusses the battle in detail in his epic poem *The Iliad*, and describes certain things—like the walls of Troy being slanted rather than straight—that were later proven to be fact based on archaeological discoveries. This suggests that Homer wrote about actual history that had been passed from generation to generation for 400 years between the so-called war and the time his poems were written. Evidence of an ancient civilization has been located in the same area Homer writes about, supporting the idea that a great city-state did exist. But why it crumbled—and if, in fact, a historic war was actually fought there—remains a mystery.

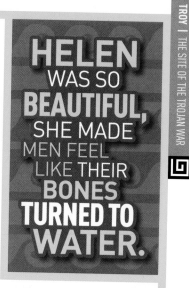

HELEN WAS SO BEAUTIFUL, SHE MADE MEN FEEL LIKE THEIR BONES TURNED TO WATER.

take that, Troy

113

IN THE GREEK CORNER...

ACHILLES

WHY HE'S WEIRD: As a baby, Achilles' mother dipped him into the River Styx in Tartarus to make him immortal. But because she held him by one heel, that heel became his one and only vulnerable spot.

WACKY TACTICS: Worried that he'd die in battle, Achilles' mom dressed him like a girl and sent him to another town for safety. (Odysseus caught on and sent him off to war anyway.)

BATTLEFIELD FACTS: Achilles killed countless Trojans throughout the war. His last battle ended tragically when Paris shot an arrow (guided by the god Apollo) into Achilles' heel.

AJAX

WHY HE'S WEIRD: Physically giant, Ajax is said to have been as tall as a tower.

WACKY TACTICS: Ajax used his supersize stature to his advantage on the battlefield. When fighting the Trojan hero Hector he picked up a huge stone that no other warrior could lift and hurled it his way, knocking Hector down—but not out.

BATTLEFIELD FACTS: Although his big size—and his huge sword and shield—fought off many enemies, Ajax could not win the one thing he wanted the most. He wound up losing a contest against Odysseus over the armor of the recently departed Achilles, and the disappointment drove him mad.

IN THE TROY CORNER...

KYKNOS

WHY HE'S WEIRD: The son of Poseidon and a mortal, Kyknos was abandoned on a beach as a baby and raised by seagulls until a fisherman adopted him.

WACKY TACTICS: Poseidon made his son invulnerable to injury from iron, meaning he could not get hurt by any sword or spear attacks. This made him almost unstoppable in battle.

BATTLEFIELD FACTS: Kyknos put up a strong fight when the Greeks first landed in Troy, slaying some 1,000 soldiers, according to some myths. It wasn't until Achilles caught onto Kyknos's special powers that he figured out another way to, uh, crush this hero with a large rock.

HECTOR

WHY HE'S WEIRD: A peace-loving prince, Hector, Paris's brother, didn't really want to go to war, but he valiantly fought in it to clean up his brother's mess—and to defend his city, home, and family from an invading army.

WACKY TACTICS: After battling Ajax for an entire day only to end up in a stalemate, Hector wound up exchanging gifts with his rival and they congratulated each other on their courage and strength. Frenemies much?

BATTLEFIELD FACTS: The leader of the Trojan army, Hector is said to have single-handedly killed 31,000 Greek soldiers. He was ultimately stopped by Achilles, seeking revenge for the death of his best friend, Patroclus.

Thebes

ΗΟΜΣ ΤΟ ΟΣDIPUS RΣX

Thebes was a thriving city-state that, at times, went to battle against other territories like Athens and Sparta. In mythology, it's known as the birthplace of Heracles and, later, brought to life in the story of Oedipus, who later became the king of Thebes.

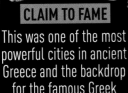

CLAIM TO FAME

This was one of the most powerful cities in ancient Greece and the backdrop for the famous Greek tragedy *Oedipus Rex* by Sophocles.

THEBES WAS A THRIVING CITY-STATE IN ANCIENT GREECE AND ALSO SERVED AS THE SETTING FOR MANY MYTHS.

8 WACKY THINGS ABOUT
THEBES

mooo!

① A COW MARKED THE SPOT

First, Zeus fell in love with a woman named Europa and kidnapped her. Then, her distraught brother, Cadmus, wanting desperately to find her, sought out an oracle to help him out. The oracle offered something along these lines: "Give up your hunt for your sister and seek out a white cow with a half-moon shape on its hide. When the cow lays down to rest, there you'll find a brand-new city." Random? Yep. But Cadmus listened, found the cow, and followed it. When the cow plopped down in a grassy meadow, Cadmus looked around and decided this was where a brand-new city would come to be. (Spoiler alert: Cadmus may have found a new town, but he never did find his sister.)

② IT HAD A DEADLY RESIDENT

As the founder of this new city, Cadmus had to locate water for his people. But there was one major problem: A deadly dragon—owned by Ares, the god of war—was guarding the freshwater fountain. Cadmus called upon Athena to help him slay the dragon, and ultimately he defeated it.

③ WARRIORS ONCE SPRUNG FROM ITS GROUND

Once the dragon was dead, Athena suggested that Cadmus plant the dragon's teeth in the soil of his new territory. Out sprung fully armed warriors from the ground. This army of *Spartoi* (meaning "sown men") began battling one another instantly. All but five of the warriors died, and those who survived helped Cadmus build the city of Thebes.

④ IT WAS A SMART CITY

Archaeological evidence shows that Thebes was an advanced city, thanks to its founder. Legend has it that Cadmus brought writing and the alphabet to his people—lessons which eventually spread throughout the world.

Αα Ββ Γγ Δδ
Εε Ζζ Ηη Θθ
Ιι Κκ Λλ Μμ
Νν Ξξ Οο Ππ
Ρϱ Σσ Ττ Υυ
Φφ Χχ Ψψ Ωω

⑤ HERACLES LIVED HERE

The mighty Greek hero Heracles is said to have been born and raised in Thebes. He eventually married Megara, the daughter of Creon, the king of Thebes.

⑥ IT WAS A MELTING POT

As a center of culture and intellect, many people from different places around Greece came to Thebes. Oedipus, the eventual king of Thebes, took up residence after having arrived from the small town of Corinth.

⑦ IT WAS GUARDED BY A WINGED SPHINX

Greek myths tell the tale of a mythical creature with a woman's head and a winged lion's body, known as the winged Sphinx of Boeotian Thebes. She stood guard at the border of the city. She'd ask all visitors to solve a riddle and would kill anyone who couldn't.

a human!

⑧ ONE KING WAS CROWNED AFTER SOLVING A RIDDLE

In *Oedipus Rex*, Oedipus becomes the king of Thebes after solving a riddle. What riddle, might you ask? It goes a little something like this: What starts out on four legs, goes to two legs, and finishes on three? The answer: A human. People begin crawling on all fours, then walk on two, then may need the assistance of a cane (the "third leg") in old age. When Oedipus offered the correct answer, the Sphinx grew so upset that she threw herself off of a cliff and died.

Athens

THE CAPITAL CITY

Athens is nestled in a lush, fertile valley between mountain ranges. It is the home of the famed Acropolis—a series of famous temples built on a rocky hill more than 3,000 years ago. It's also the birthplace of democracy, or a system of rule by the people instead of a king. In ancient times, Athens boasted the biggest navy in Greece and people came from all over the country to study at its universities and trade at its markets. Today, it's Greece's largest city, with a population of more than 3.7 million people.

CLAIM TO FAME
Athens is considered the birthplace of democracy.

RUINS FROM ANCIENT GREECE
STILL STAND TODAY, INCLUDING
THE FAMOUS ACROPOLIS, WHICH
HOUSED TEMPLES FOR THE GODS.

ATHENS

① IT HAS A NAME FOR FAME

Athens is named after the goddess Athena, who was said to have gifted its people with a bottomless supply of olive oil, wood, and food. Every four years, the citizens of Athens would honor their city's namesake with a festival known as the Panathenaia. They'd march to her temple on the Acropolis and place a new robe on her statue's shoulders.

② SERIOUSLY STATELY STATUES

The gold-and-ivory statue of Athena that stood in the Parthenon was taller than a three-story building. It's said that there were up to 2,300 pounds (1,040 kg) of gold in Athena's statue, likely made from melted coins.

③ AWESOME ARCHITECTURE

It took nine years—and some 100,000 tons of marble—to build the Parthenon. Dedicated to Athena, the Parthenon is perched high above the city. Over the years, it's been a church, a place to store ammunition, and a fortress; it has also survived earthquakes and wars.

(4) PARTY ALL THE TIME

Ancient Athens hosted more than 100 large festivals honoring the gods, goddesses, and local heroes every year—that's like a holiday every three days! People took off of work, and paraded, danced, and sang in the streets. Most festivals featured a ceremony sacrificing food or animals to the gods with the idea that the gods would help or protect them in the future.

(5) UNFINISHED BUSINESS

The still standing temple of Olympian Zeus in Athens took almost 700 years to build— and it was never actually fully completed. Many kings tried to finish it and failed, with hundreds of years going by before other leaders took on the project.

(6) OLD SCHOOL

In 387 B.C., Greek philosopher Plato founded the first ever university in Athens—which stayed open for nearly 1,000 years. But education in ancient Athens was valued at a younger level, too: Artwork on ancient vases and plates show boys in class learning to give speeches, sing, and play the lyre, while other artifacts show that students wrote on long rolls of parchment made from animal skins.

(7) GREAT GATHERINGS

Every 35 days, thousands of citizens of Athens would gather on a hill to discuss the government—a gathering also known as an assembly. The groups would grow to have up to 25,000 people, and if there weren't enough citizens at an assembly, the city police would round up more. These assemblies made all of the decisions for the city, from how to spend money to which citizens should go to the Olympics.

THE RUINS OF THE SANCTUARY WHERE APOLLO'S ORACLE IS SAID TO HAVE SPOKEN STILL STAND TODAY.

Delphi

THE CENTER OF THE UNIVERSE

Delphi was the religious center of the Greek city-states; people from all over would visit to receive guidance. Its famous oracle, the Pythia, was said to speak for the beloved god Apollo. Eventually, Delphi became a hot spot for arts, education, and trade.

CLAIM TO FAME

Delphi was considered to be the religious and cultural center of ancient Greece.

5 WACKY THINGS ABOUT
DELPHI

① CENTER STAGE

The Greeks believed that Apollo's oracle at Delphi was the center of the universe. To prove this, according to myth, Zeus released two eagles from the opposite edges of the world and commanded that they fly across Earth to meet in the middle. The eagles met up in Delphi, and Zeus placed a big rock, called the omphalos, to mark the spot.

② APOLLO RULED ...

There was no god more beloved in Delphi—or anywhere in ancient Greece, for that matter—than Apollo. His rise to fame came once he killed Python, a serpent who was terrorizing everyone on Earth by killing innocent people with its deadly bad breath. According to myth, Apollo slayed Python in Delphi—perhaps at the omphalos rock—when he was just four days old. As a result, many monuments, altars, and a huge temple were built in his honor.

③ ... AND SO DID ATHENA

Apollo may have been the top god in Delphi, but he wasn't the only immortal honored there. There was also a large shrine to Athena in front of the temple of Apollo. Experts think it was built this way by the ancient Greeks so that Athena would always protect her beloved half brother.

④ SEEING THE FUTURE

A priestess called the Pythia hung out at the temple of Apollo at Delphi, offering prophecies—or glimpses of the future—on the seventh day of every month. Believed to be speaking for Apollo, the Pythia would chew leaves from the sacred laurel tree and inhale vapors from a crack in the earth before offering her advice and visions on everything from upcoming wars to people's personal fates.

⑤ GAMES GALORE

Delphi was home to the Pythian Games, one of the most famous athletic competitions in early Greece. Started in honor of Apollo, these games featured chariot and running races as well as musical events. Similar to the Olympics, the Pythian Games were held every four years, and contest winners won laurel crowns and likely free food for life back in their hometowns.

Constellations

There are stories in the stars! Mythology is chock-full of tales of important figures—immortals and mortals alike—who were given a final resting place among the stars. Many constellations, or shapes and patterns made by groups of stars, have backstories that have been passed down since ancient times. Here's more about some of the most recognizable constellations—and the stories behind them.

URSA MAJOR & URSA MINOR

ALSO KNOWN AS: Big Bear & Little Bear

Zeus put the bears in the stars to protect them from hunters. Sometimes called the Big Dipper and Little Dipper, these are the most recognizable constellations in the sky.

Cassiopeia is actually hanging upside down in her throne, symbolized by the W shape of her constellation.

Zeus is said to have tossed the bears by their tails, giving the beasts extra-long appendages.

CASSIOPEIA

ALSO KNOWN AS: The Queen

Cassiopeia offended Poseidon by bragging that her daughter, Andromeda, was even more beautiful than the daughters of the sea god. As her punishment, Poseidon placed Cassiopeia in the heavens, trapped on her throne for all eternity.

GEMINI

ALSO KNOWN AS: The Twins

While Castor was mortal, his twin was blessed with the ability to live forever, which is why Polydeuces had to ask Zeus to strip him of his immortality so he could be with his brother in heaven.

Seeing double? This constellation symbolizes Castor and Polydeuces, the twin sons of Zeus and the mortal Leda. When Castor died in battle, Polydeuces begged Zeus to send him to heaven so he could be reunited with his twin.

Capricornus has the body and horns of a goat, but the tail of a fish.

CAPRICORNUS

ALSO KNOWN AS: The Sea Goat

This constellation represents Pan, the god of the wind and hunting, who had the head and torso of a human and the legs and horns of a goat. Myth says that when Pan tried to escape a fire-breathing monster, he tried to turn himself into a fish before plunging into the Nile River. His transformation attempt only worked halfway, and he became half goat, half fish.

ORION

ALSO KNOWN AS:
The Hunter

This constellation is named for the mighty hunter Orion, who once boasted that he could rid the Earth of all wild animals. This upset the Earth goddess Gaea, and she sent a deadly scorpion to defeat him. To avoid the scorpion, Orion jumped into the sea, and was then accidentally shot with an arrow from Artemis, who happened to be his friend. Once she realized her misstep, the goddess of the hunt begged the gods to bring Orion back to life. They refused, so Artemis placed Orion's picture in the sky so she could always have a reminder of him.

Betelgeuse, the name of a bright red star in Orion, means "armpit of the giant" in Arabic.

CANIS MAJOR & CANIS MINOR

ALSO KNOWN AS: The Larger Dog (top) & the Smaller Dog (bottom)

Orion's hunting dogs have a place in heaven right near their person. Some myths say that the pups are also positioned near the Gemini constellation, where they are waiting for scraps from the twins.

Sirius, a star in Canis Major and one of the brightest in the sky, is also known as the Dog Star.

MOST OF THE
88
OFFICIALLY
RECOGNIZED
CONSTELLATIONS
ARE NAMED AFTER
GREEK OR
ROMAN MYTHS.

AQUILA

ALSO KNOWN AS: The Eagle

Zeus's feathered friend performed different tasks in many myths. From carrying the king's thunderbolts to pecking at Prometheus's liver as punishment for stealing fire from the gods to give to humans, this hardworking eagle was given his spot in the stars.

Aquila appears close enough to the Equator that it can be seen from anywhere on Earth.

One of Delphinus's five stars is located more than 593 billion miles (954 billion km) away from Earth. Far out!

DELPHINUS

ALSO KNOWN AS: The Dolphin

Poseidon was hopelessly in love with the nymph Amphitrite—and did everything in his power to win her over. Including recruiting a cute little dolphin named Delphinus to swim over to Amphitrite and convince her to marry Poseidon. The plan worked, and the sea god honored the dolphin with a permanent home in the stars.

Sky-watchers in ancient Greece made catalogs of stars and constellations more than 2,000 years ago.

131

Nymphs

They were beautiful, mystical, and usually hung out with major gods. But nymphs were not major goddesses themselves. Rather, they're known as nature spirits of Greek mythology. And while some lived for almost 1,000 years, they were not all immortal. So just what role did nymphs play in mythology? Classified by the natural features they represented, nymphs were parked in different parts of the great outdoors. Some served to protect plants and animals; others would help sailors lost at sea. Here's a quick breakdown for your nymph knowledge:

IN FRESHWATER: OCEANIDS

Despite their name, these nymphs didn't live in the ocean, but they did protect the rivers, lakes, and ponds of the world. They were also the nymphs of clouds, winds, breezes, sunsets, and sunrises.

NOTEWORTHY NYMPHS: Metis was born a nymph but eventually became the Greek goddess of thought. Zeus fell in love with Metis, but once she became pregnant, he feared his offspring would be more powerful than him. So he turned Metis into a fly and swallowed her. A few months later, their daughter, Athena, sprung from his head (for more information on this myth, see page 47).

Myths say there were 3,000 nymphs who presided over freshwater—all the daughters of the Titans Oceanus and Tethys.

132

IN THE TREES: DRYADS

Nymphs of the woods, the Dryads presided over groves of trees and wild forests alike. Each species of tree had its own group of tree spirits, and in addition, each tree had a spirit of its own.

NOTEWORTHY NYMPHS: The Meliai, who were born from the blood of an injured Uranus, are known for looking after Zeus when he was hidden away in a cave as an infant, feeding him goat milk and honey.

A Dryad would stay alive for as long as its tree did, meaning they could live for hundreds and hundreds of years.

GOD'S SQUAD

Nymphs were often seen in the company of major gods, like Artemis, the goddess of hunting and archery. They'd join her as she traveled from land to land and cared for her deer. Pan, the god of shepherds and hunters, was often seen in the company of nymphs as he roamed through the woods. Other nymphs were said to nurture gods, like Zeus, who they cared for in the cave of Crete where he hid out from his father, Cronus.

IN THE SEAS: NEREIDS

These 50 daughters of Nereus, the god of the Mediterranean Sea, and his wife, Doris, a sea nymph, were protectors of sailors and fishermen, said to help them out when they were having trouble on the open water. The Nereids, who were also attendants of Poseidon, could be seen riding waves or laying out on the rocky shore.

NOTEWORTHY NYMPHS:

One of the Nereids, Amphitrite, was the wife of Poseidon, the Olympian god of the ocean. She's known as the female personification of the sea.

The Nereids were often shown riding on the backs of dolphins or mythological half-horse, half-fish creatures known as Hippocamps.

CALL OF THE SIRENS

Not all nymphs were joyous and helpful. The Sirens, for example, were half-women, half-bird sea nymphs known for their reckless behavior. This chorus would sing songs that distracted sailors, causing them to crash on the rocks of their islands. The Sirens would then eat the sailors. Naughty nymphs.

MODERN MYTHOLOGY
BUGGING OUT

Nymphs in real life? It's not exactly what you think. At their very early stages of life, some insects are known as nymphs—tiny bugs that already look like the adult form of their species, minus the wings. (They'll eventually grow those.) These bugs borrow their name from mythology: Naiads, the nymphs of aquatic insects, get their name from the water nymphs that inhabited rivers and springs.

IN THE MOUNTAINS: OREADS

The nymphs of mountains, hills, rocky slopes, and caves, Oreads helped travelers navigate dangerous mountain passes and hills. They'd also help gods like Artemis hunt deer, chase wild boar, and bring down birds of prey with their arrows.

NOTEWORTHY NYMPHS: Echo, an Oread nymph of Mount Helicon, was cursed by the goddess Hera, who rendered her unable to speak except for the ability to repeat the last words said by someone else.

Unlike most other nymphs, Oreads were immortal.

Morph-ology

MYTHIC SHAPE-SHIFTERS

THETIS

For many figures in Greek mythology, changing shape was no big deal. Whether they wanted to escape an enemy, impress someone, or just blend into the background, transformations were pretty common in myths. While gods could easily and instantly morph from one shape to another, humans were not so lucky. Once a god transformed them into another object—usually as a punishment for crossing them—humans were usually stuck in that shape forever.

FROM THIS

TO THAT

TALE OF TRANSFORMATION:
Just call him persistent Peleus! This mortal king was completely enamored by Thetis, a sea nymph. But she wanted nothing to do with him and managed to escape his advances by switching into different shapes. She'd change into a body of water, the wind, a tree, a bird, and more. With the help of the wise centaur Chiron, Peleus was finally able to outwit Thetis's shape-changing powers, and the two married in front of all of the gods. They later welcomed a son, the great warrior Achilles.

A BIRD, FIRE, WATER, WIND, A TIGER, A LION & A TREE

FROM THIS

DAPHNE

TO THAT

A LAUREL TREE

TALE OF TRANSFORMATION: Struck by one of Eros's arrows, the god Apollo fell deeply in love with the river god Peneus's beautiful daughter Daphne. But, like many gods, Apollo was far too persistent in his attempt to win Daphne's heart. One day, as he chased her in the woods, Daphne called out to her father, Peneus. She begged that he change her form so she could escape Apollo's inevitable capture. Within seconds, stiff bark began covering her body and face. Her hair become emerald green leaves, her arms branches, and her feet, like roots, stuck firmly in the ground. Apollo stood mesmerized as he watched his love transform into a tree. Once he realized he would never have Daphne as his wife, he plucked leafy branches from her limbs and made a crown. From that point on, he wore the laurel crown proudly, a reminder of his lost love.

TALE OF TRANSFORMATION:
Myth tells us that Apollo, the god of the sun, was born on the island of Delos and became an adult in just four days. When he was ready to leave the island, he turned himself into a dolphin and swam toward the shore. His destination? The city of Delphi (short for *delphinos*, the Greek word for "dolphin"), said to be named after Apollo's spirit animal.

APOLLO

FROM THIS

TO THAT

A DOLPHIN

ARTEMIS

Zeus is the king of shape-shifting: In various myths, he turned into a bull, an eagle, a cuckoo bird, a serpent, a rain shower of gold, and more—all to woo women.

FROM THIS

A DOE

TALE OF TRANSFORMATION:
Artemis, the goddess of the moon and the hunt, used her shape-shifting powers to bring down a pair of badly behaved twin giants known as the Aloadae. The two sons of Poseidon had plans to storm Mount Olympus and steal the goddesses Hera and Artemis for their own. But before they could do that, the quick-thinking Artemis changed herself into a doe. When the brothers saw the beautiful deer bounding before them, they aimed their spears to hunt her down. Artemis disappeared in an instant, and the Aloadae wound up throwing their spears at each other instead, fatally wounding one another. Oh, deer.

TO THAT

Muses

CREATIVE INSPIRATIONS

Talk about a sister act! Mythology tells the stories of the Muses, nine sister goddesses who inspired people in the arts and sciences. The daughters of Zeus and Mnemosyne, the goddess of memory, the Muses were often called upon to offer guidance and good vibes for poets, musicians, artists, and writers. The Muses were trained by Apollo in song and dance, and lived on Mount Olympus, where they often entertained the gods with their musical gifts. However, they'd also travel down to Earth to work their individual Muse magic on mortals, like transforming simple shepherds into famous poets and inspiring artists to create masterpieces.

CALLIOPE

ALSO KNOWN AS:
Protector of Epic Poetry

NEVER LEFT HOME WITHOUT HER ...
Writing tablet and stylus

A-MUSE-ING FACT:
The oldest of the Muses, Calliope was called upon for her beautiful words and eloquent speech. She helped inspire Homer as he wrote his epic poem *The Odyssey*.

CLIO

ALSO KNOWN AS:
Protector of History

NEVER LEFT HOME WITHOUT HER ...
Trumpet in one hand and a book in the other

A-MUSE-ING FACT:
Clio is credited with guiding many ancient Greek historians to assist in their retelling of famous events.

ΜΕLΡΟΜΕΝΣ

ALSO KNOWN AS: Protector of Tragedy

NEVER LEFT HOME WITHOUT HER ...
Tragic mask and bat

A-MUSE-ING FACT:
While she was often the creative force behind dramatic tragedies in theater, Melpomene, also known as the song-stress, was called upon to create beautiful lyrical phrases in songs.

ΣUTΣRΡΣ

ALSO KNOWN AS: Protector of Music

NEVER LEFT HOME WITHOUT HER ... Flute

A-MUSE-ING FACT:
Euterpe is said to have invented the flute and other wind instruments. Musicians would call upon her to inspire and guide them as they wrote their compositions.

THALIA

ALSO KNOWN AS:
Protector of Comedy

NEVER LEFT HOME WITHOUT HER ...
Comedy mask and instrument

A-MUSE-ING FACT:
Thalia may have been funny, but she had a serious side, too: Aside from inspiring laughs in the theater, she is also credited with discovering geometry.

ΣRATO

ALSO KNOWN AS: Protector of Love Songs and Poems

NEVER LEFT HOME WITHOUT HER ...
Lyre, love arrows, and bows

A-MUSE-ING FACT:
Her name comes from the Greek word *eros*, which refers to the feeling of falling in love. In fact, she often traveled with Eros, and the two of them would shoot arrows at people, causing them to fall in love with the first thing they laid eyes on.

URANIA

ALSO KNOWN AS:
Protector of Astronomy

NEVER LEFT HOME WITHOUT HER ... Globe and pencil

A-MUSE-ING FACT:
The mythological inventor of astronomy, Urania inspired men to explore the sky. She's also the Muse behind astrology, or the practice of looking at the stars to predict the future.

POLYHYMNIA

ALSO KNOWN AS:
Protector of Sacred Poetry

NEVER LEFT HOME WITHOUT HER ... Lyre

A-MUSE-ING FACT:
Known as the more serious, conservative Muse, Polyhymnia inspired deep thinkers. She may have also invented meditation, as she's often depicted leaning on a column, grounded in deep thoughts.

TERPSICHORE

ALSO KNOWN AS:
Protector of Dancing

NEVER LEFT HOME WITHOUT HER ...
Laurel wreath crown and harp

A-MUSE-ING FACT:
Terpsichore—named after the Greek word meaning "delight in dancing"—loved to have fun. When she wasn't cutting it up on the dance floor, she was playing her harp, which she helped popularize.

143

The Hall of Horrors

MYTHICAL MONSTERS

The monsters of myth weren't anything you'd ever want to mess around with. With freaky features like poisonous breath, snakes for hair, and multiple heads, they were certainly the stuff of nightmares. But for all of their ferociousness, most of these monsters couldn't scare away some of the most famous and powerful gods and mortals. Myths tell terrifying—but triumphant—tales of the heroes who battled these beasts. Read on to find out more about some of the scariest monsters in mythology.

SPHINX

HIDEOUT: The city of Thebes

MONSTER FILE: The Sphinx terrorized the city of Thebes, killing all those who could not solve its riddle. Finally, Oedipus solved the riddle and the city was saved. (Read more about the riddle on page 119!)

The Sphinx had the body of a lion, the head of a woman, and the wings of an eagle.

The fire-breathing Chimera had a snake for a tail, a goat's body, and a lion's head.

CHIMERA

HIDEOUT: Ancient Turkey

MONSTER FILE: When the warrior Bellerophon was sent to destroy the Chimera, he hopped on his winged horse, Pegasus, and shot poisonous arrows at her from above. But the Chimera refused to fall. So Bellerophon attached lead to his spear, and risked it all to get close enough to plunge the spear into the Chimera's tough skin.

POLYPHEMUS

HIDEOUT: A cave on the island of Sicily

MONSTER FILE: En route back to his home after the Trojan War, Odysseus and his crew bumped into this big guy on the island of the Cyclopes (also known as Sicily). There, they camped out in a cave and snacked on some sheep lingering nearby. These sheep just so happened to belong to Polyphemus, who went after Odysseus and his men, nabbing two of them before the rest were able to escape by blinding the Cyclops and sneaking out.

Any mortal who looked at Medusa, who had hissing snakes for hair, instantly turned to stone.

MEDUSA

HIDEOUT: The rocky island of Sarpedon at the edge of the Earth

MONSTER FILE: Medusa wasn't born a monster. Rather, she was turned into a wretched woman with terrifying tusks, wings sprouting from her back, and a head full of snakes as a punishment by the goddess Athena. Ugly as she was, Medusa wasn't unlovable: Poseidon became smitten with her and brought her down to live with him in his sea kingdom.

TYPHON

HIDEOUT: A cave in ancient Greece

MONSTER FILE: The youngest son of Gaea and the brother of Zeus (who ultimately slayed this beast with his thunderbolt), Typhon had 100 snake heads that sprang from his shoulders. Sometimes called the father of monsters, Typhon and his wife Echidna's brood included equally horrific offspring, including the Chimera, Cerberus, the Nemean lion, and the Sphinx.

Typhon's eyes flashed fire and his hands and body were a mass of hissing snakes.

SCYLLA

HIDEOUT: On the banks of a narrow stretch in the ocean

MONSTER FILE: The only way for Odysseus to get home was through a narrow stretch of sea, where monsters waited on either side. Scylla had a perch on one side, snapping her many jaws at the ships attempting to pass by. They carefully rowed first past Charybdis—the other monster who whipped the ocean into a swirling frenzy—before approaching Scylla. She swooped down and gobbled up six men, but Odysseus and the rest of his crew kept rowing. They eventually made it through the strait, and were able to continue toward their destination.

Scylla had six snakelike heads and would feast on sailors she snapped up as they rowed by.

NEMEAN LION

HIDEOUT: The countryside of the kingdom of Nemea

MONSTER FILE: As part of the to-do list he needed to complete to become immortal, the famous Greek hero Heracles was tasked with taking down this mega-size lion, who stalked the fields of Nemea. After realizing that his arrows were useless against the beast, Heracles trapped the lion in a cave. There, he was able to finish off this big cat with his hands.

MINOTAUR

HIDEOUT: Labyrinth of Crete, a Greek island

MONSTER FILE: The Minotaur stalked the maze in Crete, munching on the young children—also known as tributes—sacrificed to him every nine years. It wasn't until the hero Theseus—on a mission to become the king of Athens—had a courageous and bloody battle with the beast that the Minotaur's deadly reign finally ended.

LERNAEAN HYDRA

HIDEOUT: Murky waters of the swamps of Lerna and the surrounding countryside

MONSTER FILE: Another monster Heracles had to hunt down on his quest to become immortal, the Hydra was hard to stop. Heracles had to sear each of the Hydra's necks with a burning spear to prevent them from growing back, cutting off the last head and burying it under a boulder to finally lay the beast to rest.

Half man, half bull with deadly horns, the Minotaur was actually the pet of King Minos.

Gigantomachy

REVENGE OF THE TITANS

CLAIM TO FAME
This was the war between a tribe of giants and the Olympian gods.

WHY IT'S WEIRD

To fight the gods, the giants threw huge boulders and burning trees toward Mount Olympus.

A GIANT PLAN

The giants—also known as the gigantes—were the oversize offspring of Gaea and Uranus. These behemoths are sometimes portrayed as having the scales and tails of a dragon. They may not have been pretty, but they were definitely powerful. And they hoped to use their strength to overthrow the gods. This was no easy task, of course, but the giants had, well, *big* plans.

REVENGE OF THE TITANS

So what did the giants have against the gods, anyway? A lot of it had to do with their mom. Still stewing over the gods' takeover of the Earth from the Titans during the Titanomachy, Gaea urged her brood to seek revenge. The giants themselves were frustrated about having to obey the laws that Zeus put into place, so they were more than happy to set their sights on destruction.

Getting to that castle in the clouds would be the first tough task to tackle. The giants couldn't fly, so they had to figure out an alternative route. Using their superhuman strength, they stacked three mountains on top of each other, and climbed the pile of peaks like a ladder. Now that's some supersize smarts!

DOWN AND OUT

Meanwhile, on Mount Olympus, the gods heeded the prophecy of Hera, queen of the gods. She had been warned that the gods could only win this war if a mortal participated in the battle. So they called up the hero Heracles to help fight off the approaching enemies.

The giants fought with their muscles, hurling huge boulders and burning trees toward Mount Olympus. Zeus retaliated by launching giant thunderbolts their way. Heracles then stepped in, jumping on one of the most powerful giants, Alcyoneus, knocking him down (and out). Finally, to slay the giant of all giants, Ephialtes, Apollo shot an arrow into his eye, according to one myth. And because Heracles had to finish him off, he shot another arrow at Ephialtes. Game over.

UNDER PRESSURE

After that pivotal point, the rest of the giants ran off, ending the bloody battle. The gods buried the bodies of the slain giants beneath mountains, leading the ancient Greeks to believe that volcanic eruptions and earthquakes were caused by the rumblings of the spirits of these "trapped" giants, resting not-so-peacefully.

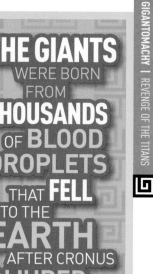

THE GIANTS WERE BORN FROM **THOUSANDS** OF **BLOOD DROPLETS** THAT **FELL** TO THE **EARTH** AFTER CRONUS **INJURED URANUS.**

let me out!

149

Centauromachy

AN ΣPIC BATTLΣ

CLAIM TO FAME
This was a clash between the centaurs and the Lapiths, a legendary tribe of humans.

WHY IT'S WEIRD Half-horse, half-man creatures tussling with humans? Enough said.

POWERFUL FIGHTERS,
CENTAURS
RIPPED TRUNKS OF TREES
OUT OF THE GROUND
TO HURL AT THEIR ENEMIES.

MODERN MYTHOLOGY
ALL ABOUT ART

The Centauromachy is one of the most common scenes depicted in art. Many famous artists, including the great Michelangelo, created sculptures, paintings, and other artifacts featuring images of the Lapiths tussling with the centaurs. The ancient Greeks even chose to add scenes from the Centauromachy on the outside of the Parthenon in Athens. You can still see some of these marble sculptures, known as metopes, on exhibit in museums.

NIGHTMARE NUPTIALS

Weddings are usually a happy occasion. But according to one myth, a certain wedding between two mortals became more of a nightmare than a dream when a group of unruly centaurs showed up. While some centaurs, like Chiron, were extremely civilized and smart, others had the habit of causing trouble wherever they roamed. At this particular wedding, one of the centaurs attempted to run off with the bride. The celebration turned chaotic, and what wound up happening is known as the Centauromachy.

During the fight, weapons became pretty much whatever wasn't nailed down—cups, candles, and tables. In the violent struggle, the centaurs also crushed their opponents with rocks. Once the centaurs brought down a Lapith named Caeneus, the hero Theseus stepped in to protect the Lapiths. Theseus ultimately slayed the centaur Eurytion, and the rest of the beaten-down centaurs retreated.

A BARBARIC BATTLE

Though a brief war, the Centauromachy has tons of significance. Ancient Greeks believed that this myth represented the struggle between civilized behavior (the Lapiths) and wild behavior, or barbarism (the centaurs). In fact, the word "barbarian" originated in ancient Greece to describe all non-Greek-speaking people.

TOTAL TRANSFORMATION

Caeneus, a Lapith, was one of the most notable victims of the Centauromachy. Born a girl, he was turned into a man—and a warrior invulnerable to weapons—by Poseidon. After the centaurs crushed him by piling trees on top of him, Caeneus transformed once more. This time, as a bird who simply flew away from the bloody battle.

151

The Amazons

THE FIERCEST FEMALES

CLAIM TO FAME

They represented an entire nation of warrior women.

WHY THEY'RE WEIRD

Myths say that when an Amazon had a baby boy, she'd send him to his father to be raised.

No boys allowed! At least that's the way the Amazons preferred things. This tribe of fierce females—said to be the daughters of Ares, the god of war, and the minor goddess Harmonia—lived on the edge of the world, without men. As beautiful as they were deadly, you definitely didn't want to mess with these women. They were not only skilled on horseback, they were also aces at fighting with bows, spears, and axes. Myths of these brave, independent, and lovely warriors raised questions about whether women could be equal to men.

THE AMAZONS
MEASURED
5 FEET 6 INCHES
(1.7 M)—
EXCEPTIONALLY
TALL
FOR THE TIME.

REAL-LIFE AMAZONS

Were there any Amazons in real life? Experts say it's possible. Amazons were thought to be solely mythological until archaeologists unearthed burials of real women warriors believed to live in western Asia. These nomadic hunters lived in small all-female tribes, where they rode around on horseback and hunted with bows and arrows. Talk about girl power!

LOVE AND WAR

The Amazons pop up in mythology quite a few times, most notably when they go to battle against some of mythology's strongest heroes. For example, there's the story of Heracles, who was tasked with stealing the belt of the Amazon queen Hippolyta as one of his 12 labors (see page 88), which ultimately led to an encounter between the hero and the Amazons.

Perhaps one of the most famous mentions of Amazons in mythology is in a war against Athens. While helping out his buddy Heracles, the hero Theseus locked eyes on the Amazon Antiope. He wound up taking her back home to marry her, ruffling the feathers of the other Amazons. When Theseus became the ruler of Athens, they sought revenge for their stolen sister and embarked on a vicious battle versus the Athenians.

The Amazons appeared yet again in the tales of the Trojan War, when they sided with the Trojans in an effort to defeat the Greeks. Myth says that the hero Achilles eventually slays the Amazon Penthesilea—only to regret that move once he takes off her helmet and falls in love with his beautiful victim. Love hurts.

MODERN MYTHOLOGY WONDER WOMEN!

Fierce, strong, and statuesque: That's the stuff superheroes are made of. In fact, the Amazons of Greek mythology inspired a fictional female warrior better known as Wonder Woman. Also known as the Amazon princess Diana of Themyscira, daughter of Queen Hippolyta, Wonder Woman sports golden armor, a shield, and wields an ax, making her a throwback to the ancient version of an Amazon ... with a twist.

Theban Cycle

A COLLECTION OF ANCIENT POEMS

How do we know all that we do about mythology? Most of these stories come from the vivid imagery in ancient writing that's been passed on from generation to generation.

Some of the most prominent stories in mythology feature the city of Thebes, the birthplace of the hero Heracles (to read more about Thebes, check out pages 116–119). These tales were originally told in a collection of epic poems, written some 2,500 years ago, also known as the Theban Cycle. While the actual poems were lost or destroyed over the years, their words made a lasting impact: Many famous Athenian writers used the poems as inspiration for their own work, some of which went on to become central works of ancient Greek literature. The Theban Cycle includes stories about three generations of a cursed family. Here are the plots of these poems in a nutshell.

SPOTLIGHT ON SOPHOCLES

Thanks to the works of ancient Greek poets and writers, we probably know more about Greek mythology than any other ancient myths. While Homer and Hesiod gave us glimpses of the most common myths, most of what we know about the story of Oedipus stems from the words of ancient Greek playwright Sophocles. Drawing from ancient works like the Theban Cycle, he wrote a total of 123 plays, including *Oedipus Rex* and *Antigone*. But Sophocles wasn't just a writing whiz: An accomplished soldier, he led the Greeks to victory at sea in a battle against the Persians. Another awesome accomplishment? He lived until he was about 90 years old!

THE OEDIPODEA

THE WRITER: Cinaethon, an unknown poet from Sparta

THE PLOT: This gives background on Oedipus, who meets a Sphinx on the road to Thebes, and is challenged to a riddle. Oedipus gets the riddle right and becomes king of Thebes.

THE THEBAIS

THE WRITER: Unknown, although many people attribute it to the poet Homer

THE PLOT: The story between Oedipus's twin sons, Eteocles and Polynices, and their unsuccessful attempt to take over the city of Thebes. The twins can't decide who should reign over Thebes, so they decide to take turns as king. When Eteocles refuses to give up the throne, his brother gathers a small army known as the Seven Against Thebes. The two wind up killing each other with swords in battle.

THE EPIGONI

THE WRITER: Either Antimachus of Teos, an early Greek poet, Homer, or a Homer impostor

THE PLOT: The sequel to the battle between Eteocles and Polynices, this highlights the Epigoni (meaning "next generation" in Greek), or the children of the Seven Against Thebes. This time, the plan to attack Thebes works, and the Epigoni are able to avenge the death of their fathers.

SO EPIC!

Epic isn't just an adjective to describe something extra amazing. Rather, when it comes to writing, an epic is a long, narrative poem that typically tells tales of heroes, intense adventures, and fantastic feats. Homer's *The Iliad* and *The Odyssey* are both considered epic poems.

It takes 18 hours to read *The Odyssey* out loud from cover to cover.

Game On!

THE ANCIENT OLYMPICS

THE 1896 OLYMPICS OPENING CEREMONY

WHY IT'S WEIRD

In the earliest Olympic Games, competitors competed without any clothes on.

The Olympics' origins are similar to many other ancient Greek festivals: It was a way to honor their gods. The first Greek Olympics, held in the city of Olympia in 776 B.C., celebrated Zeus. There, athletes from throughout Greece as well as distant lands would compete in events such as wrestling, boxing, long jump, javelin, discus, and horse-drawn chariot racing. Even if certain city-states were at war against each other, a truce would be called prior to the Olympics so that the athletes could travel to Olympia in safety. This ancient event inspired our own Olympic Games.

BIG LOVE FOR ZEUS

The ancient Greeks didn't mess around when it came to honoring Zeus. Looking over the games in Athens was a giant temple dedicated to the king of gods in Olympia, including a huge statue of Zeus. Towering at the height of a four-story building and covered in gold and ivory, the statue took 12 years to build. One of the seven wonders of the ancient world, the statue stood tall for centuries before being destroyed some 1,500 years ago.

A FEAT OF STRENGTH

Forget barbells and burpees: One famous ancient Greek Olympian, Milos of Croton, lifted a cow to get stronger! He first began carrying around a baby calf every day, and as the cow grew, Milos gained more strength. Eventually, his whole village would turn out to watch the local strongman walk around with full-size cow on his shoulders. Now that's one way to moove!

MODERN MYTHOLOGY
HEAVY MEDAL

Before there was Usain Bolt, there was Leonidas of Rhodes. The superstar of the ancient Olympics, Leonidas was an undefeated track star who won a record-setting 12 events over three games some 2,000 years ago. What's more? He likely raced in heavy battle gear—including a helmet, breastplate, and shield—in temps topping 90°F (32°C). That almost makes today's track events look like a walk in the park. Almost.

A TALE OF TWO MYTHS

There's more than one myth about how the Olympic Games got started. Here are two that have stood the test of time.

MYTH 1: PELOPS THE CHEATER

Were the Olympics originated by a cheater? Oddly enough, some experts think so. The story goes that Pelops, a grandson of Zeus, was hoping to woo a princess named Hippodamia. Standing in his way? Hippodamia's father, King Oinomaos of Pisa. The king ruled that anyone who wanted Hippodamia's hand in marriage would have to beat him in a chariot race. Pelops was up for the challenge—sort of. To guarantee a win, he first had a friend secretly remove the linchpins in the king's chariot. When the race went off, Oinomaos's chariot fell apart and he lost the race. The cheater Pelops won his bride, then started up the Olympic Games to celebrate his so-called victory.

MYTH 2: HERACLES THE HERO

As a nod for helping him out as he tackled his 12 labors to become immortal, Heracles instituted the Olympic Games in honor of his father, Zeus. It's said that the hero taught men how to wrestle, and measured out the stadium as the length of the 600-foot (183-m) footrace. Event winners received wreaths of olive branches from trees said to be planted by Heracles.

Romans

ROMAN MYTHOLOGY

If imitation is the sincerest form of flattery, then the Romans must have thought the Greeks were pretty amazing. This admiration led to the Romans borrowing the myths of the ancient Greeks and adapting them to their own gods. A thousand years after the Greek myths began circulating, the Romans came up with their own versions of the same stories. And even though the names changed, the stories stayed relatively the same—except they're set in ancient Rome. Here's a list of gods with both Greek and Roman names.

GREEK NAME	ROMAN NAME	ROLE
GAEA	TERRA	GODDESS OF THE EARTH
URANUS	CAELUS	GOD OF THE SKY
CRONUS	SATURN	FATHER OF ZEUS, YOUNGEST SON OF URANUS
ZEUS	JUPITER	KING OF GODS
HERA	JUNO	GODDESS OF MARRIAGE
POSEIDON	NEPTUNE	GOD OF THE SEA
HADES	PLUTO	GOD OF THE UNDERWORLD
DEMETER	CERES	GODDESS OF THE HARVEST

NAME THAT PLANET

The Greek gods have been around for, well, ever. So why do the Roman gods, who came along much later, get the glory when it comes to the planets? Because the ancient Romans named them! After observing the planets' movements and appearance, those ancient astronomers gave them names that matched a similar god or goddess:

Mars, the color of blood, reflects the god of war; Venus, which shines the brightest, is named for the goddess of beauty; Mercury, the fastest-moving planet, is named for the messenger of the gods. In fact, Earth is the only planet in our solar system whose name is not plucked from mythology—derived from English and German, it simply means "ground."

GREEK NAME	ROMAN NAME	ROLE
PERSEPHONE	PROSERPINA	GODDESS OF THE UNDERWORLD
HERMES	MERCURY	MESSENGER OF THE GODS
ATHENA	MINERVA	GODDESS OF WISDOM
ARTEMIS	DIANA	GODDESS OF THE HUNT
APOLLO	APOLLO	GOD OF MUSIC AND MEDICINE
HEPHAESTUS	VULCAN	GOD OF THE FORGE
APHRODITE	VENUS	GODDESS OF LOVE
EROS	CUPID	GOD OF LOVE
ARES	MARS	GOD OF WAR
DIONYSUS	BACCHUS	GOD OF MERRIMENT AND THEATER

Famous heroes like Heracles, Theseus, and Achilles may stand apart from the crowd when it comes to phenomenal feats, but Greek mythology also mentions other impressive individuals who pushed boundaries and displayed their fair share of wit, bravery, or brilliance. These unsung heroes may not have made major headlines, but their myths are certainly worth a mention.

ORPHEUS

A magical musician, Orpheus helped save Jason and the Argonauts from the song of the Sirens. When the dangerous sea nymphs let out their enchanting—but evil—call, he played his own, more powerful music, and saved the crew from certain death.

Orpheus's music could charm wild animals and make rivers stand still.

PELASGOS

The clever king of the Arcadians, Pelasgos taught his people to eat nuts, like acorns, off of trees to avoid going hungry or getting sick by eating potentially poisonous roots and leaves.

ORION

A super-skilled hunter, Orion rose to fame on the island of Chios by driving all of the wild beasts off the island. He later became a hunting partner to the goddess Artemis, who accidentally killed him with an arrow.

Orion could walk on water, a gift from his father Poseidon.

PERDIX

The young nephew of the famous inventor Daedalus is said to have come up with some some clever ideas himself, including the world's first drawing compass and saw. Myth says he created the saw out of a snake's jaw!

After he was hurled from a cliff by his jealous uncle, Athena changed the boy into a bird. *Perdix* is the Greek word for "partridge," a type of bird.

A DIFFERENT KIND OF HERO

Not all Greek heroes are perfect. Some even make huge mistakes. In literature, these are known as tragic heroes: characters with a fatal flaw who are doomed to fail despite their best intentions. One example of a tragic hero? Icarus, whose father, the great inventor Daedalus, crafted two pairs of wings out of feathers and wax. As he fit Icarus with the wings, Daedalus warned his son to stick by his side while they flew. But an arrogant Icarus soared higher and higher until he was so close to the sun that the wax on the wings began to melt. Icarus plummeted to the ground and died. Today, his story is still used as a warning about the dangerous effects of being overconfident.

She-roes

WOMΣN WHO ROCKΣD

There are plenty of heroines in Greek mythology. However, unlike their male counterparts, most of these women are not depicted as going out on quests, engaging in combat, or seeking immortality. Some mythological heroines boast honorable qualities like bravery, wisdom, or dignity—while others made the ultimate sacrifice by giving up their own lives for the greater good.

ATALANTA

Atalanta could outrace and outwrestle any man.

Abandoned as a baby and then raised by bears and a group of hunters, Atalanta grew to be one of the fiercest and fastest female warriors ever. She led a team of some of the best hunters in Greece to slay a vicious bear ravaging the city of Calydon.

NAUSICAA

When a bedraggled Odysseus shipwrecked on her island on his long journey back from the Trojan War, the brave young princess Nausicaa found him, cared for him, and introduced him to her royal parents, who helped him on his way.

ARIADNE

Madly in love with the hero Theseus, Ariadne played a key role in helping him defeat the monstrous Minotaur. How? By giving him a ball of thread so that he could find his way out of the Minotaur's maze. Yet despite her above-and-beyond acts, Theseus didn't really return the love and wound up ditching her on the island of Naxos.

MEDEA

Medea, a princess and sorceress, tapped into her special powers to help Jason secure the Golden Fleece, like putting fire-breathing bulls to sleep so Jason could slip by them. She also gave him advice on how to overcome other tasks in order to grab the Golden Fleece.

IPHIGENIA

After Iphigenia's father angered Artemis by hunting down one of her sacred deer, the goddess stalled the ocean's winds—making it impossible for the Greeks to sail their ships toward Troy to fight in the Trojan War. Sacrificing Iphigenia to please Artemis allowed the Greeks to advance toward Troy.

PENELOPE

The daring and patient Penelope, wife of Odysseus, outwitted her suitors for years while her husband was on his decade-long journey back from the Trojan War to his home in Ithaca. She occupied herself by weaving a large cloth every day, only to unravel it each night and start over again.

PSYCHE

The goddess Aphrodite had no love for Psyche, who was married to her son Eros. So she broke up the marriage and sent Psyche to the Underworld to complete four tasks to reclaim her son's love. These included sorting a huge pile from seeds, grabbing a handful of wool from the Golden Fleece, filling up a container at the River Styx, and bringing Aphrodite a box of Persephone's beauty ointment. The last task lead Psyche to fall into a deathlike sleep until Eros brought her up to Olympus, where Zeus made her immortal.

Psyche is the Greek word for "soul."

163

STUMP YOUR PARENTS

MYTHOLOGICAL POP QUIZ

When it comes to mythology, are your parents masters—or is it all Greek to them? Give them this quiz to see if they know their stuff!

1 The Minotaur was a creature who had the body of a human and the head and tail of a _____.

a. fish
b. dragon
c. lion
d. bull

2 True or false? The Parthenon was built to honor Zeus.

3 Pegasus was a mythological creature that looked like a horse with _____.

a. horns
b. wings
c. three tails
d. blue eyes

4 As the queen of the Titans, Rhea was also known as _____.

a. mother of gods   c. Mother Earth
b. sister of gods   d. Big Mama

5 True or false? The Greeks believed the sun was pulled across the sky by Apollo's chariot, led by golden horses.

6 Hydra, the largest constellation in the night sky, is named after which kind of mythological monster?

a. A water snake   c. A three-headed dog
b. A fire-breathing dragon   d. A woman with snakes for hair

7 True or false? The story of Peter Pan may have been inspired by Greek mythology.

8 What did Hephaestus make for the gods?

a. Pandora, the first mortal woman in the world
b. Hermes' winged hat and sandals
c. Eros's silver bows and arrows
d. All of the above

HERO MATCHUP

Being a Greek hero is no easy task. Match some of the fiercest figures in mythology with their famous feat!

BELLEROPHON

ODYSSEUS

PERSEUS

HERACLES

PROMETHEUS

166

THE FEATS

1 This quick-thinking warrior beheaded the monstrous Medusa—a Gorgon whose gaze could turn any mortal to stone. How'd he do it? By watching her in the mirrored reflection of his shield instead of making direct eye contact.

2 He slayed many monsters, including the Minotaur, who liked to feast on children. He later became the king of Athens.

3 To earn his own kingdom, he set sail along with 50 friends in search of the Golden Fleece from a magical lamb. After overcoming many harrowing hurdles, they ultimately captured the fleece.

JASON

4 This brawny hero ticked off a to-do list of 12 nearly impossible labors—including slaying horrific monsters—in order to gain immortality.

5 He stole fire from Zeus and brought it to mankind, giving humans the ability to advance by cooking for themselves. As punishment, Zeus chained him to a rock, where a bird pecked at his liver every day until he was rescued.

THESEUS

6 He sealed his status as a mythological hero by slaying the fire-breathing Chimera, a monster with the head of a lion, the body of a goat, and the tail of a dragon. He also waged a fierce battle against the Amazons.

7 A celebrated warrior, he helped the Greeks triumph in the Trojan War and then endured a very long journey home. Facing monsters, Amazon warriors, rough seas, and more, he used his courage and cleverness to reach his final destination.

ANSWERS:
1. Perseus
2. Theseus
3. Jason
4. Heracles
5. Prometheus
6. Bellerophon
7. Odysseus

10 WACKY FACTS

ABOUT GREEK MYTHOLOGY

1 On the third day of the ancient Olympics, **100 COWS** were sacrificed to honor Zeus and other gods.

2 **THERE'S A BONE** in your spine that's named after **ATLAS, THE GREEK GOD WHO HOLDS UP THE SKY.**

3 THE GREEK NAME FOR **THE 12 OLYMPIANS** IS DODEKATHEON.

4 Director George Lucas got many of his ideas for *Star Wars* from Greek mythology.

5 GREEK GODS **DIDN'T** HAVE **BLOOD.** Instead, it's said that **A GOLDEN SUBSTANCE** called **ICHOR** flowed through their veins.

6 The famous battle between Zeus and the Titans is said to have taken place on the Greek island of Mykonos—one of the world's top tourist destinations today.

7 **GREEK MYTHS** WERE ALL WRITTEN AS **LONG POEMS.**

8 The Greek god **DIONYSUS** is often shown WITH A SQUAD OF SATYRS: HALF-GOAT, HALF-MAN CREATURES who played the flute.

10 **JELLYFISH** are named after **MEDUSA** in many languages, including **SPANISH, RUSSIAN, FRENCH & GREEK.**

9 **IN 1969,** THE UNITED STATES NAMED THEIR FIRST MISSIONS TO THE MOON **APOLLO,** AFTER THE GREEK GOD.

WHICH GREEK GOD(DESS) ARE YOU?

Do you love being the center of attention or are you more of a behind-the-scenes kind of kid? Do you dream about epic adventures or do you prefer to keep things more chill? Take this personality quiz to find out which ancient Greek god or goddess you're most like! It's OK if your result doesn't fit your personality—this is just for fun!

1 Summer is just around the corner, and it's time to sign up for camp. What kind do you pick?

a. Sports camp. You're super competitive.
b. Cooking camp. You love being in the kitchen.
c. Rock camp! You love to sing and play instruments.
d. Adventure camp. Climbing trees, hiking, exploring ... bring it on!

2 You're packing for a weekend trip away with your family. What's the first thing you stash in your bag?

a. Sports gear. Your baseball mitt, a bathing suit, a basketball, a lacrosse stick ... whatever fits!
b. Snacks! You don't go anywhere without a tasty treat.
c. Your iPod and headphones. You can't live without your tunes!
d. A pair of binoculars. You never know what you might spy!

3 What's your favorite animal?

a. Cheetah
b. Monkey
c. Owl
d. You love them all … it's hard to pick just one.

4 It's talent show time at your school. What's your act?

a. A gymnastics routine
b. A cooking demonstration
c. A song and dance
d. None of the above. You prefer to be behind the scenes, not on stage.

5 You have a day off from school. How will you spend the time?

a. Playing pickup basketball with the kids on your street
b. Making cupcakes and decorating them with your siblings
c. Practicing playing your new guitar
d. Riding your bike with your friends

MOSTLY A'S

Hermes. Just like Hermes, you are athletic and social, and love a good game. Whether it's being part of a sports team or challenging your sister to a Scrabble battle, you are always up for a little friendly competition. But as much as you love to win, you don't take things *too* seriously. For you, it's all about fun first!

MOSTLY B'S

Demeter. Your favorite spot is in the kitchen, cooking up a feast for your family or baking sweet treats for your friends. Like Demeter, the goddess of harvest, you enjoy providing tasty bites for those you love. You also have a green thumb and can grow just about anything in your backyard garden, and your big, bold personality is simply blooming with life.

MOSTLY C'S

Apollo. You're definitely tuned in to music—just like Apollo! Playing instruments comes naturally to you, and you're always fiddling around with a guitar, teaching yourself to play the piano, or singing along to your favorite song. Gathering together with your friends and family? You're the first one to entertain them with a song or dance. Encore!

MOSTLY D'S

Artemis. Hiking, biking, or just hanging in a hammock: You love being in nature and spend as much time as you can in the great outdoors. Like Artemis, you're crazy about animals—and they love you a bunch back. Spending time playing with your puppy or cuddling kittens would be your perfect way to spend a day, *paws* down.

SPIRIT ANIMALS

In Greek mythology, each Greek god and goddess has specific symbols assigned to them, including sacred animals. From soaring birds to snakes with wings, these companions appear alongside the gods in art, often play pivotal roles in myths, and sometimes represent certain personality traits that are characteristics of the gods.

ZEUS

SPIRIT ANIMAL: Eagle

Zeus's constant companion? A giant eagle that served as his personal messenger. This wasn't just any big bird: Some myths say it was actually a mortal king whom Zeus transformed into an eagle as a form of punishment.

HERA

SPIRIT ANIMAL: Peacock

This flashy and fancy bird is definitely fit for a queen: It's known for its pride and strutting around flaunting its beauty, much like Hera was apt to do. (And all of those eyes on its tail feathers kept an eye on Hera's husband, Zeus.)

HADES

SPIRIT ANIMAL: Screech-owl

The ancient Greeks believed that the screech of this bird signified impending death, linking it to the god of the Underworld.

POSEIDON

SPIRIT ANIMAL: Horse

It's said that Poseidon created the first horse out of waves to impress the goddess Demeter, who had asked him to craft the most beautiful animal in the world.

ATHENA

SPIRIT ANIMAL: Owl

Athena is often shown with an owl on her shoulder that was said to give her advice and whisper words of wisdom in her ear.

173

ARES

SPIRIT ANIMAL: Vulture

Ares, the god of war, is linked to these scavenging birds. They're often seen as a bad omen, haunting the battlefield and feeding upon the bodies of the dead.

ARTEMIS

SPIRIT ANIMAL: Hunting dog

This master hunter didn't go anywhere without her four-legged companion, who also represented her loyalty to her friends and those who surrounded her in the forest.

APOLLO

SPIRIT ANIMAL: Wolf

Like a lone wolf, Apollo often traveled solo and kept his distance from other gods and mortals. Some myths even say that the only way to communicate with him was through oracles or his father, Zeus.

APHRODITE

SPIRIT ANIMAL: Turtle dove

Turtle doves, the birds of love, followed Aphrodite everywhere she went, even pulling her chariot across the heavens.

HERMES

SPIRIT ANIMAL: Tortoise

Even though Hermes had amazing speed, he was often associated with this slow-moving reptile since he made the original lyre from its shell.

DEMETER

SPIRIT ANIMAL: Snakes

A pair of winged serpents pulled Demeter's chariot. They are said to represent her feminine wisdom.

GLOSSARY

AMAZONS:
A female-only tribe of warriors who lived on the edge of the world.

AMBROSIA:
A mythical mixture known as the food of the gods; it may have consisted of honey, cheese, olive oil, fruit, and barley.

ARGO:
A 50-oared ship used by the hero Jason on his journey to find the Golden Fleece.

CENTAUR:
A mythological creature with the head, arms, and torso of a man and the body and legs of a horse.

CENTAUROMACHY:
A fight between centaurs and men.

CERBERUS:
A three-headed dog that served as the guard of the gate to the Underworld.

CONSTELLATION:

A shape or pattern made by a group of stars, many of which have backstories that have been passed down since ancient times.

CURETES:

Tiny soldiers who kept watch outside of the cave where Zeus was hidden away from his father, Cronus.

CYCLOPES:

A race of one-eyed giants.

EPIC:

A long poem, usually describing the deeds and adventures of heroic or legendary figures.

GIGANTES:

The oversize offspring of Gaea and Uranus, sometimes portrayed as having the scales and tails of a dragon.

HECATONCHEIRES:

Massive beasts with 50 heads and 100 arms who were the children of Gaea and Uranus.

IMMORTAL:

A divine being who has the ability to live forever.

LAMPADEDROMIA:

An ancient Greek race celebrating the gods where participants passed a torch from one runner to another.

LAPITHS:

A legendary tribe of humans who fought with the centaurs during the Centauromachy.

LYRE:

A harplike instrument created by Hermes out of a tortoise shell and stretched-out sheep guts.

MINOR GODS:

Gods who had less power than the Olympian gods and laid claim to very small territories—like a stream or a single tree.

MORTAL:

A being who is subject to death; in mythology, humans, heroes, and monsters were mostly mortals.

MOUNT OLYMPUS:

The place believed to be the home of the 12 major gods.

MUSES:

Nine sister goddesses who inspired people in the arts and sciences.

MYTHOLOGY:

A collection of stories, or myths, especially one belonging to a particular religious or cultural tradition.

NYMPH:

A humanlike female spirit bound to a particular place in nature.

ORACLE:

Someone who offered wisdom; a future-teller.

PITHOS:

A clay jar used in ancient times; thought to be Pandora's box that contained all of the evil in the world.

POMEGRANATE:

Also known as "the fruit of the dead"; Persephone ate its seeds while in the Underworld, forcing her to live there for half the year.

PLOUTONION:

An area where the ancient Greeks would make sacrifices to the god of the Underworld.

SPELT:

An ancient strain of wheat that Demeter, the goddess of grain, is credited with discovering and teaching others how to grow and harvest.

SYMPLEGADES:

A narrow area of enormous moving rocks and crashing waves that Jason and the Argonauts had to pass through during their journey.

STAFF:

A magical stick with snakes wrapped around it. It could control and heal mortals. Also known as a caduceus, it was often used by Hermes.

TARTARUS:

The darkest, deepest pit under the earth where Zeus would banish his enemies.

THEBAN CYCLE:

A collection of 2,500-year-old epic poems written about the city of Thebes.

TITANS:

The offspring of Gaea and Uranus who ruled the Earth until they were overthrown by Zeus.

TITANOMACHY:

The fierce 10-year battle where Zeus and his siblings defeated their father, Cronus, and the other Titans.

TRAGIC HEROES:

In literature, these are known as characters with a fatal flaw who are doomed to fail despite their best intentions.

TRIBUTES:

Seven girls and seven boys offered up as food for the Minotaur, a heinous half man, half bull who lived in a maze known as the Labyrinth.

TRIDENT:

A three-pronged spear used by Poseidon.

UNDERWORLD:

The mythical home of the dead, located beneath the earth and ruled by Hades.

home sweet home

Boldface indicates illustrations. If illustrations are included within a page span, the entire span is **boldface.**

INDEX

INDEX

INDEX

PHOTO CREDITS

CREDITS

This book would not have been possible without the creative brilliance and careful, thoughtful editing of Ariane Szu-Tu and Becky Baines or the insightful guidance of Dr. Diane Cline in the Department of History at George Washington University. My gratitude to all of you for your kindness, patience, and advice.

Thank you to my family, including my parents and sisters for believing in me and reading just about every word I've ever written.

Finally, to Eamon, Nora, and Nell: May life lead you on many epic journeys. And remember: You have the strength and smarts to slay all of the monsters.

To Mark: You truly are my hero ... and that's no myth.
—S.W.F.

ISBN 978-1-338-32189-0

12 11 10 9 8 7 6 5 4 3 2 1   18 19 20 21 22 23

Printed in the U.S.A.   40

First Scholastic printing, September 2018

Designed by Sanjida Rashid
Illustrations by Chip Wass

The publisher would like to thank the team who helped make this book possible: Ariane Szu-Tu, associate editor; Becky Baines, executive editor; and Sarah J. Mock, senior photo editor.